DISCOVER··NATURE
at the
Seashore

DISCOVER · NATURE
at the
Seashore

Things to know and things to do

Elizabeth P. Lawlor

with illustrations by Pat Archer

STACKPOLE
BOOKS

Published by
STACKPOLE BOOKS
Cameron and Kelker Streets
P.O. Box 1831
Harrisburg, PA 17105

Printed in the United States of America

First Edition

10 9 8 7 6 5 4 3 2 1

Library of Congress Cataloging-in-Publication Data

Lawlor, Elizabeth P.
    Discover nature : at the seashore : things to know and things to
do / Elizabeth P. Lawlor. — 1st ed.
        p.   cm.
    Includes bibliographical references and index.
    Summary: Introduces the three types of seashore and the creatures
and features of each. Presents related experiments.
    ISBN 0-8117-3079-4
    1. Seashore biology—Juvenile literature. [1. Seashore biology.]
I. Title
QH95.7.L358   1992
508.314'6—dc20   91-17260
                                                           CIP
                                                           AC

This book is dedicated
with fondest memories
to my father,
the late John J. Phelan, who inspired me,
and
with deepest affection
to my friend and colleague
Dr. Francis X. Lawlor, who encouraged me.

There was a child went forth every day,
And the first object he looked upon, that object he
    became,
And that object became part of him for the day or a
    certain part of the day,
Or for many years or stretching cycles of
    years.
The early lilacs became part of this child,
And grass and white and red morning-glories, and . . .
The horizon's edge, the flying sea crow, the
    fragrance of salt marsh and shore mud,
These became part of that child who went forth every
    day, and who now goes, and will always go forth
    every day.

Walt Whitman, "There Was a Child Went Forth"

TABLE OF CONTENTS

ACKNOWLEDGMENTS

This book got its start when I was encouraged to write about nature by Trudy Sharp when she was president of the Greenwich, Connecticut, chapter of the National Audubon Society. My first efforts were sponsored by Greenwich Audubon as a monthly newspaper column called "Nature's Notebook," which was published in *The Greenwich Time*. The information sections of many of the chapters appeared in a preliminary form in these columns. In this connection, I want to thank Bob Pellegrino, features editor of *The Greenwich Time*. Another thank-you goes to Jan Linsky and Bill Ross, subsequent presidents of Greenwich Audubon, for their continued support and encouragement.

I'm grateful for the helpful insights and suggestions that were offered by Dr. Miriam Balmuth and Dr. Sally-Ann Milgram, two of my colleagues at Hunter College, City University of New York. I also want to thank my dean, Dr. Hugh J. Scott, and my chairperson, Dr. Mae Gamble, for facilitating the sabbatical leave from Hunter College that gave me the time to research and prepare this book for publication.

I am also grateful to the many science specialists who took the time to review my work. The fact that many of them never met me is a testimony to their spirit of cooperation and dedication to their fields of study. In alphabetical order, they are Dr. Barbara Dexter, Division of Natural Sciences, SUNY-Purchase; Dr. Michael LeFor, Department of Geography, University of Connecticut; Dr. Robert Singletary, Department of Biology, University of Bridgeport; Dr. Charles Yarrish, Department of Biology/Marine Sciences at Groton, University of Connecticut.

Other reviewers who read parts of the manuscript and offered helpful suggestions were Ted Gilman, Environmental Education Specialist, National Audubon Society Center, Greenwich, Connecticut; Lisette Henrey, Director of Outreach Programs, the Bruce Museum, Greenwich, Connecticut; Matthew Lerman, Marine Science Educator, Beach Channel High School, New York City; Bruce Miller, Outreach Program Teacher, the Bruce Museum, Greenwich, Connecticut; Rick Schreiner, Executive Director of the Long Island Sound Task Force, Stamford, Connecticut; Marianne Smith, Curator of Natural Sciences, the Bruce Museum, Greenwich, Connecticut.

I am also indebted to the library staffs of the following institutions: Hunter College of the City University of New York; Salisbury State University, Salisbury, Maryland; Norman Hall Library of the University of Florida, Gainesville, Florida; and the Greenwich Library, Greenwich, Connecticut.

I extend a very special thanks to two of my mentors and friends, Dr. Mary Budd Rowe of Stanford University, Palo Alto, California, and Professor Emeritus Willard J. Jacobson, Teachers College, Columbia University. I cannot omit thanking my science educator–husband, Dr. Francis X. Lawlor, former Curator of Natural Science at the Bruce Museum, and skipper of the ketch *Jolly Dolphin*, which faithfully carried us along the coast from the wilds of Quebec to Key West in search of the plants and animals of the intertidal zone. I also want to thank my editor at Stackpole Books, Sally Atwater, for guiding me through new waters. To these and many other generous professionals who have shared their expertise and to all of the little creatures of the intertidal zone who have taught me and delighted me, thank you.

INTRODUCTION

This book is for people who want to get closer to nature. It is concerned with both knowing and doing. This book is for the young, for parents, for students, for teachers, for retirees, for all those with a new or a renewed interest in the plants and animals living at the edge of the salty sea. Getting started as a naturalist requires a friendly, patient guide. This book is not a field guide; it is intended to gently lead you to the point of knowledge and experience where various field guides will be useful to you. When you have "done" this book, I hope that you will feel in touch with the dwellers of the intertidal zone.

THE STRUCTURE OF THE BOOK

Each chapter introduces you to a common, easily found plant or animal. You will learn about its unique place in the web of life and about the most fascinating aspects of its life-style. This information summarizes the major points of interest in the scientific research available on each topic. Each chapter also provides you with activities—things you can do to discover for yourself exactly where each living thing is found, what it looks like, and how it behaves and survives.

At the seashore there are three different habitats or environments: the rocky shore, the salt marsh–mud flat, and the sandy beach–dunes. The book is divided into three corresponding parts. Each part features the major plants and animals found in that habitat. In the first part of each chapter, you will find the important facts about a particular living thing, including some amazing discoveries that scientists have made. You will learn the common names of living things and their scientific names, which are usually Latin. In the second part of each chapter, called "The World of. . . ," you will be guided through a series of observational and exploratory activities. This personal "hands-on" involvement with plants and animals is certainly the most important of all learning experiences. This is how you will really discover what life between the tides is all about, something that no amount of reading can give you.

As you read and investigate, you will begin to understand how fragile the seaside communities of living things are in a time of crisis. You will inevitably encounter the effects of man's presence. I hope that you will become concerned, not in a vague way, but in specific, practical ways. This is exactly how people like the author Rachel Carson became aware, became concerned, and began to make a difference for the future of the environment. We still have a long way to go.

HOW TO USE THIS BOOK

Feel free to start reading at any point in this book. For instance, if you are thinking of taking a vacation on the rocky coast, you will want to read about barnacles, sea stars, or seaweeds. Then, when you are getting ready to go, read the section following this one, "What to Wear and What to Bring." When you actually visit the shore, take the book with you. Prepare for your observations and explorations by reading first and by gathering the specific items you will need. You will find suggestions in the "What You Will Need" part of each chapter. This part of each chapter also tells you which specific science-process skills are developed in each activity. Do take the suggestion that you keep a field notebook. You can begin this process by making notes in the spaces provided in this book.

My great hope is that this book will be only a beginning for you. I have suggested other readings, keyed to each chapter, to help you learn more than this book can provide. In a sense, when you go out into the marsh, onto the mud flats, down on the rocks when the tide is low, into the sand dunes, you will go beyond all the books. Once you get started, Nature herself will be your guide.

WHAT TO WEAR AND WHAT TO BRING

What to Wear. Don't explore the rocky shore or the marsh in bare feet. Wear sneakers that fasten tightly; otherwise you may lose them in the mud.

On the rocky shore, you especially need sneakers that will give you a good grip on the slippery rocks. You also need to protect your feet from the razor-sharp cutting edges of barnacle cones. Some people like to wear a pair of gloves and long pants to protect their hands and legs from barnacles, too. When the water is too cold to wear sneakers, it's good to have a pair of rubber boots or waders.

A long-sleeved shirt gives good protection from the biting insects that live in the salt marsh, but you may want to stay away from blue. Some research indicates that blue is a color that attracts mosquitoes. A soft, crushable hat with a wide brim will protect your face from the sun and cast a helpful shadow on objects you're examining. Of course, an explorer's kit would be incomplete without sunglasses and a tube of sunscreen. And don't forget to bring a towel.

What to Bring. You'll need very little equipment to become fully involved in the hands-on activities that appear in the Explorations section of this book. But I do suggest that you put together a basic kit that will include a few essentials. The first thing you'll need in your kit is a field notebook. I generally use a spiral-bound, five-by-seven-inch memo book. Include several ballpoint pens and pencils. Since many of the explorations will involve taking measurements of some plants and animals, put a six-inch flexible ruler or tape measure in your kit. Include a small magnifier or hand lens (10x). Nature centers generally stock plastic lenses that are very good and usually inexpensive. You may also want to have a bug box in your basic kit. This item is simply a small, see-through box, a one-and-one-half-inch cube, with a magnifier permanently set into its lid. It's a handy item for holding such creatures as beach fleas, shrimps, and other types of amphipods. With it, you can capture, hold, and examine a creature without touching it or harming it.

All of the contents of your basic kit can easily fit into a medium-sized Ziploc bag. You can carry the kit in a backpack, a bicycle basket, or the glove compartment of a car.

Basic Kit:
field notebook
pens and pencils
ruler or tape measure
magnifier
bug box

Although it is not essential to have a pair of binoculars, they are guaranteed to add to your joy of discovery. Some inexpensive binoculars, however, provide poor image quality; choose a pair made by a major camera manufacturer. Compact binoculars of seven or eight power are usually best for use in the field.

You'll also find that having a camera will add interest to your study of plants and animals.

There are other items that you may need occasionally but that don't have to be included in the basic kit, such as a bucket, a glass pie plate, plastic containers and bottles of various sizes with lids, scales, a scoop net, a watch with a second hand, sticks, rubber bands, sandpaper, a sketch pad, and waterproof markers.

You may also find that you need a three-ringed, loose-leaf notebook in which you can enter, in an expanded form, the information collected in the field. The extra time that this requires gives you an opportunity to reflect on what you saw and to think through some of the questions raised during your explorations. During this quiet time, you can also consult your reference books and field guides for additional information. This more or less permanent notebook is an ideal place to file photographs taken in the field.

PART I
THE ROCKY SHORE

I N OUR EFFORTS to understand any other nation, we recognize the importance of knowing the history of that nation. Exactly the same principle applies to an understanding of a natural habitat. The marsh, beach, or rocky shore that you visit also has a history, a long history reaching back perhaps tens of thousands of years. Knowing something about its history will help you to understand a particular habitat as a home for various plants and animals.

When we consider the special habitat known as the rocky shore of the Northeast or the Northwest Coast, we must reach back millions of years to envision the volcanic origins of the gray granite with its sparkling flecks of quartz and mica, or of the dark, heavy basaltic rocks that make up this type of shore. The geological formations have their origins in the fiery interior of the planet. The boulders that you see are fragments of molten magma that was long ago forced from great depths.

For millions of years, the granite and basalt that we see coated with algae and barnacles were buried thousands of feet beneath the earth's surface. The history of the movement of these rocks, with the slow, inexorable drift of the great tectonic plates that make up the surface of the earth, is not the history of greatest interest to the student of life in the tidal zone. We must pursue the more recent history of the rocky coast.

Scientists divide the history of the planet into great chunks of time called *eras*, which are divided into smaller units called *periods*, which are in turn divided into *epochs*. We are in the Cenozoic era, which began about 65 million years ago. We are also in the Quaternary period of that era, which began about 1.8 million years ago. Finally, we are in the Recent, or Holocene, epoch, which began ten thousand years ago. The epoch just prior to ours was the Pleistocene; it was during this epoch that our rocky coasts were given the features that result in the spectacular beauty we observe today.

The most important events that occurred during the Pleistocene epoch were the repeated formations of continental and alpine glaciers, which covered much of the earth. Although a great deal of information about the formation and movement of continental glaciers is still unknown, scientists have been able to build models of them by studying existing glaciers and by observing evidence of how the ancient glaciers carved out the soil and rock. This research suggests that the centers of ice making in North America were located in Labrador, north of Newfoundland; in the regions west of the Hudson Bay in the

Northwest Territories; and in Baffin, Elizabeth, Victoria, and other islands close to the North Pole. As the icy masses grew, they moved southward, fused, and formed the great ice field of the epoch. They stretched a four-thousand-mile width over Canada, dropped into the northern central and northeastern region of the United States, and extended seaward far into the Atlantic.

Geologists no longer speak of this time in the earth's history as *the* great ice age. They no longer believe that one vast sheet of ice grew, covered the continent, and remained until conditions changed, causing the ice to retreat. Today, geologists believe that there were four significant glacial advances during the Pleistocene epoch. Evidence further suggests that there were interglacial periods between these advances, during which the ice retreated. Geologists think that the ice may even have completely disappeared two or three times.

In order of appearance, the four glacial periods in the Pleistocene epoch were the Nebraskan, the Kansan, the Illinoisan, and the Wisconsin. The first three names reflect the southernmost point reached by those glaciers. The most recent ice advance bears the name of Wisconsin, where today scientists study glacial debris deposited in a forest bed near Manitowoc. Dating felled logs with radioactive carbon has disclosed that the end of the Pleistocene in this region was about eleven thousand years ago. Research also suggests that we are presently in an interglacial period and that our climate is colder than it was in some of the earlier intervals between glaciers.

As the Pleistocene glaciers advanced and retreated, each vigorously kneaded the earth, scraping, gouging, and rending vegetation and rock formations from mountaintops and from the walls of river valleys. Each glacier scooped massive amounts of earth and boulders from its path, thus rearranging many of the geological features formed by previous glaciers of the epoch. The sprawling ice sheets that caused this remodeling of the earth's surface were massive. They were over a mile thick. It is estimated that one acre of ice, one mile thick, weighed about 7.5 million tons, which translates to 3 billion tons per square mile. Since the earth's crust is elastic, it yielded to this great weight, and entire land masses were depressed, as the glaciers advanced from their origins in the Canadian ice fields.

As the most recent ice mass of the Pleistocene began to retreat, its melt water filled the depressions that it had gouged from the earth's crust. Lakes and ponds formed. The gigantic quantity of melt water caused the level of the sea to rise as much as several hundred feet. As it rose, the sea covered hills and flooded valleys.

The northeast coast, including New Hampshire, Maine, and the Canadian maritime provinces, is famous for the thousands of islands that stud its waters.

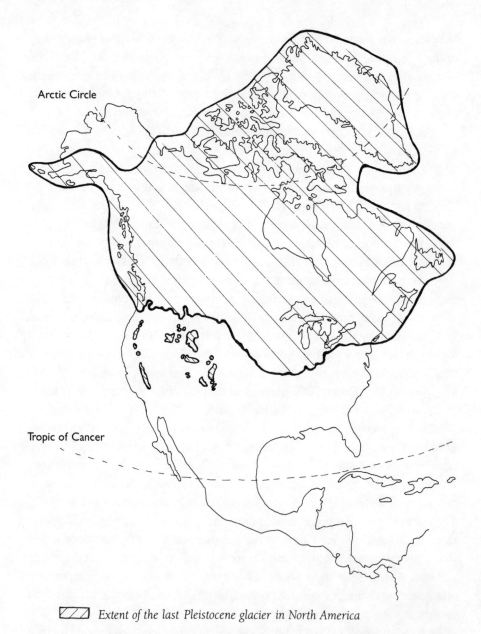

Arctic Circle

Tropic of Cancer

▨ *Extent of the last Pleistocene glacier in North America*

Rounded by glacial action and submerged by an estimated three-hundred-foot rise in sea level, these once majestic mountains and their numerous submerged ridges are now the ingredients of a sailor's nightmare as he threads his boat through the granite maze along the often fogbound coast. Other geological features, so characteristic of this coast, are the numerous coves and bays, such as Casco Bay, Muscongus Bay, Penobscot Bay, Passamaquoddy Bay, and the Bay

THE ROCKY SHORE

of Fundy, which developed when the long, lanky arms of the rising sea slowly reached inland and flooded the newly formed river valleys.

Thus there are many geological processes involved in the formation of the irregular coastline of the Northeast: the abrading action of the moving glaciers, the elasticity of the earth's crust, and the inundation of these depressed land masses by a rising sea level. For these reasons, scientists refer to the coastal northeast as a "drowned coast."

The west coast, similarly flooded when melting glaciers raised the level of the world's oceans, is also a drowned coast, but it was not directly shaped by glaciers. The west coast was given its present characteristics by volcanic action and the uplifting effects of the Pacific and American tectonic plates that collided there. The power of these formative processes is made dramatically and vividly clear in such relatively recent events as the explosion of Mount St. Helens and the violent earthquakes in Alaska and California.

If you stand on cliffs that overlook the rocky coast, the general impression is that this coastline is a wild and barren wilderness that supports only a few rugged life forms, such as the lichens that paint the bare rocks beneath your feet. Pine and spruce, clothed in the thick, heavy cobwebs of old-man's beard (*Usnea barbata*), and granite outcrops seem to be the only things produced by the thin soil. However, as you shall see, the rocky shore is actually extremely prolific.

Its bold headlands and the thousands of protected coves and bays are teeming with life. The tough, erosion-resistant granite provides a firm base upon which a vast variety of living things can establish a foothold. The smaller rocks and crevices offer shelter to additional organisms that manage to live their lives amid swirling tidal currents and the often brutal bashing from angry waves.

The rise and fall of the tide along this stretch of coastline may be as much as forty feet, although a range of ten to twenty feet is more common. Tidal action of this magnitude produces bands, or zones, that vary tremendously, depending on certain physical conditions, such as exposure to wind and light, the length of time the zone is covered by the sea, temperature, and salinity. The living things that occupy these zones are specially adapted to live in each band and show great diversity in life-styles. In the pages that follow, you will be exploring these many life forms that lie hidden from all but the inquisitive and persistent.

As you explore the rocky coast, try to find some of the many other life forms that live here, in addition to those outlined in the essays and activities that follow. You'll be fascinated by the soft-bodied "squishies," such as sea grapes, northern sea pork, and other sea squirts. Look for their enemies, the sea slugs, relatives of the snail. Dainty colonies of tiny animals grow on rocks, seaweeds, and snail shells, while worms cling tenaciously to life on the rocky shore. The list of clingers and creepers could go on, but why not discover for yourself how they live, how they are dependent on each other, and how the patterns of their lives weave a tapestry of exquisite beauty?

CHAPTER I

The Barnacle

A PRISONER ON THE ROCKS

Barnacles are clinging, ubiquitous animals of the rocky shore. They're probably best known because of the aggravation they cause saltwater sailors who try to keep boat bottoms clean and slick for the next race. Others who know these animals quite well are barefoot beachcombers. Perhaps you, too, have encountered the cutting edge of the barnacle cone and received wounds that were slow to heal.

Through the ages, these curious creatures, the dominant animals of the intertidal zone, have been cursed and much maligned. If you take a close look at these little beasts, however, you must admire the fascinating characteristics that have made them so highly successful in an extremely rigorous environment. Their success is due to some interesting survival strategies.

The barnacle is an animal whose adult body is completely imprisoned by a circle of rigid plates made from calcium carbonate, which is extracted from seawater and then secreted by the animal. The fortress thus produced is a hard, cone-shaped structure that resembles a small volcano. Covering the crater of the volcano are two pairs of movable plates, which are controlled by muscles within the cone. The action of these muscles can open the plates for feeding and reproductive purposes and close the plates to protect the soft-bodied animal within from predators and from the drying effects of exposure to sunlight and air during low tide.

For centuries, because of their hard outer shells, barnacles were thought to be mollusks, related to mussels, snails, and clams. However, about one hundred years ago, careful observation of the adult and the developing larval forms revealed that barnacles are crustaceans. They are actually relatives of crabs and lobsters. In the first stage of their development, after hatching from eggs set

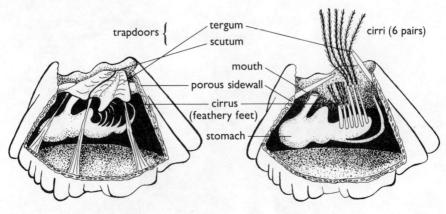

trapdoors { tergum / scutum — cirri (6 pairs)

mouth

porous sidewall

cirrus (feathery feet)

stomach

Internal structure of a barnacle (simplified)

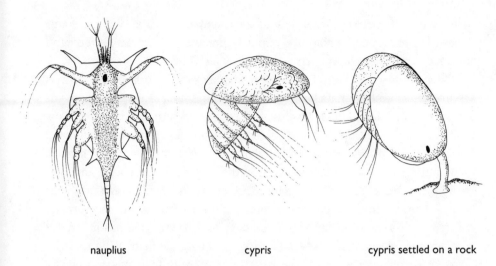

| nauplius | cypris | cypris settled on a rock |

Stages of barnacle development

adrift in the sea, the young barnacles are called nauplii. (See the accompanying diagram for the stages in their development.) With the help of a microscope or a very strong hand lens, you could see that, at this stage, they resemble a teardrop with three pairs of legs, one big eye, and a pair of horns. At this point in their development, their relationship to the other crustaceans is obvious.

Barnacles are hermaphrodites, which means that each individual is both male and female, but as a rule, barnacles don't self-fertilize. Biologically speaking, that would be a desperate move, one that is used only when a barnacle happens to be isolated from others of the same species. However, it's a desirable alternative in an emergency.

Fertilization generally takes place when one barnacle, acting as a male, extends a long, slender tube through the opening of a neighbor's shell and deposits sperm. The fertilized eggs develop inside the second barnacle. After hatching, the typical motile crustacean larvae are set free to fend for themselves amid the plankton. Of the several million larvae thus released in the waters by each barnacle, only a relative few ever reach maturity.

The nauplii are voracious eaters and weak swimmers. At this stage, their sole objectives are to eat, develop, and build energy reserves. After several weeks of growing, the larvae undergo another period of reorganization and emerge as cyprides (see diagram). In this new shape, with substantial stores of energy, the larvae spend all of their time looking for a suitable place to settle down and begin home building. As they search, the cyprides crawl around, head down, feeling their way along the rocky shore with a pair of sensory antennae. Barnacles in well-established colonies release chemicals into the water, which the larvae sense through their antennae. The ability of the young to detect the location of a mature group is important, since it is a reproductive advantage for the developing barnacles to join a colony.

Upon finding the desirable location, the sucker-like tips of the cypris's antennae attach the animal's head to a rock, a ship's hull, or whatever happens to provide a firm foundation. Now the task of cone construction begins. As any do-it-yourself home builder knows, this task demands enormous amounts of energy, so the cyprides continue to draw from the carbohydrate supply stashed away during their nauplii days. Glands at the base of the barnacle's antennae begin to secrete a mixture of calcium carbonate, which together with some protein, hardens in the water. Once cemented to the foundation, the barnacle will remain attached for the rest of its life. This amazing glue has fascinated many groups of scientists, especially those in the dental field. Within twelve hours or so of securing itself, the larva undergoes its final metamorphosis. During metamorphosis, the six pairs of jointed, crustacean-style walking legs become feeding appendages, or cirri. The feather-like cirri, covered with tiny hairs, give the barnacle one of its more formal names, cirriped (Lat. *cirrus*, curls of hair, and *pedis*, foot). Also during this final stage of development, the young barnacle begins to build the familiar cone that will cover and protect its soft body. The barnacle, now with a firm purchase on a hard substrate, becomes the world's only fixed crustacean!

As the tide rolls in, the food-laden water flows over the barnacle. At this time, the animal opens the movable plates (scuta and terga) that cover the

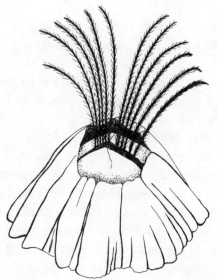

Barnacle feeding

THE ROCKY SHORE

crater of its cone. As if on command, its feathery legs, the cirri, acting like plankton nets, rhythmically sweep the water, capturing very tiny bits of food to transfer to its mouth. It has been estimated that cirri can be extended and retracted approximately 140 times per minute.

After several hours, the tide waters return to the sea. To avoid being baked by the summer sun or frozen by winter winds, the barnacle closes up shop, often with an audible snap of the scuta and terga. With the top plates closed, the barnacle can tolerate long periods of dryness, exposure to rain, or freezing temperatures.

Two naturalists, Louis Agassiz and Thomas Huxley, described barnacles as "shrimp-like animals that stand on their heads in limestone houses kicking food into their mouths." Others have not been so kind. Nevertheless, when you see barnacle carpets covering every rock in the intertidal zone, you know the clinging crustaceans are certainly biologically successful.

Although barnacles have superb defenses, they are not immune from attack by other animals. Any abundant form of life represents an abundant source of nourishment and energy for other life forms. Barnacles that live in the lower range of the intertidal area are prey to mollusks, such as the dog whelk, and sea stars. On the pacific coast, the channeled drills and emarginate drills prey upon barnacles. Various fish have powerful jaws adapted to crushing the barnacle. You may observe sandpipers using their slender, pointed beaks to feed upon barnacles. Oystercatchers are also birds that snack upon these tasty morsels attached to the intertidal rocks. Barnacles are therefore an important link in the food chain, because they provide a transfer of energy from the plankton to the vertebrates.

THE WORLD OF THE BARNACLE

What you will need
basic kit
thermometer
bucket
vinegar
medicine dropper
nail polish

Science skills
observing
recording
measuring

OBSERVATIONS
Where to Find Barnacles. Barnacles can be found growing in profusion on the rocks of the intertidal zone. At low tide when the rocks are uncovered, you will notice a distinct white band that appears beneath the black zone where

slippery blue-green algae flourish. Look carefully at this white band and you will discover the barnacle colony. Note the location of barnacles relative to the other plants and animals that make their homes on the rocks and boulders of the intertidal zone. (See Chapter Note 1 for additional guidance.) Draw a picture in your notebook indicating the relative position of the barnacle zone and the additional bands created by other living things.

Look for barnacles in other areas, such as dock pilings and jetties. Do the barnacles grow in the same relative position in these places as they do on the intertidal rocks? Did you find the same animals and seaweeds in these places as you did on the rocks? Make a list of the animals that share a dock piling with barnacles. Did you find barnacles growing in other places, such as on mussel shells?

Structural Adaptations of Barnacles. Find a spot where there are an exceptionally large number of barnacles. Because they occur in such profusion, crowding within a population is a serious problem for them, but barnacles have an interesting way of adjusting to these conditions. Do you observe anything unusual about the shapes of the densely packed barnacles? This is a structural adjustment that some of the barnacles have made. (See Chapter Note 2 for information on structural adjustment.)

External Structure of the Barnacle. Find a good-sized barnacle that has attached to a rock or a shell that you can pick up and easily examine with your hand lens. Can you see into the cone, or are the trapdoors closed? Is it white or ivory? Does it look green? Is there algae growing on it? Is it stained some other color by some material dissolved in the water? Are the plates that make up the cone smooth, or are they rough and wavy? Look closely at the plates that cover the opening of the barnacle cone. Your hand lens will help. How many plates are there? Draw a barnacle and include the plates that make up the cone and the trapdoors.

Now that you have had a really close look at one barnacle, look around at some others. Do you see differences in color, shape, texture, or the number of plates? Generally, different species of barnacles will form separate colonies because of their special reproductive methods. How many different types of barnacles did you discover? Write a description of the different species you found and make drawings in your field notebook. In what part of the intertidal zone did you find each type? Don't forget to identify the portion of the rocky shore where you made your observations. Is the area exposed to ocean waves or is it in a protected cove or estuary? Include the name of the area and its location, so that you can find it again if you need to.

There are several species of barnacles that make their home along the shore of the Atlantic and Pacific coasts, as well as along the Gulf of Mexico. With the appropriate field guide in hand, go on a barnacle hunt to see how many different types you can find. To add to the fun, take a few friends along with you.

EXPLORATIONS

Barnacles Feeding. Barnacles feed in an extraordinary way. Find a rock with several barnacles on it, and place it in a bucket containing some seawater. After a few minutes, the barnacles may begin to feed. What do you notice? Use a magnifier to observe the tiny "feet"; then describe how they work during the feeding process. How do the plates that cover the opening of the cone function during the feeding process?

The Influence of the Tide on Feeding. Do barnacles feed whenever they are covered with seawater, or is their feeding closely bound to the time of high tide? On a day that you can spend some time barnacle watching, check the local newspaper to find out when high tide occurs. At the level of mean high water, find some small barnacle-covered rocks. An hour or so before the incoming tidal waters are due to cover them, put the rocks into a bucket of seawater. When do the barnacles begin to feed? Are barnacles opportunists, grabbing a bite of plankton whenever they get a chance, or does their feeding appear to be closely linked to high tide?

Water Temperature and Feeding Rate. Water temperature affects many aspects of marine life. For example, it is one of the conditions that prompt barnacles to spawn. How does water temperature affect the rate at which barnacles feed? You can observe their feeding rate by noting how rapidly the barnacles wave their feet in and out of the cone. A good place to observe this action is in a tide pool, since the water remains trapped in the rock pond even at low tide. Take the temperature of the water in a tide pool as the tide begins to fall. Record it on a chart similar to the one below.

At each recorded temperature, count how many times per minute a cone opens and the tiny "feet" sweep the water for plankton. You can count for fifteen seconds and multiply that number by four. Repeat this several times, and calculate the average rate of sweeping for a specific temperature. Record it on your chart. Is the feeding rate the same for the other barnacles in the tide pool?

Allow some time to pass and then take the temperature of the water in the tide pool again. How do you explain the temperature difference? Find the average feeding rate of barnacles at this new temperature. As the water continues to warm, repeat this process at several different temperatures. What did

TEMPERATURE AND ITS EFFECT ON
THE RATE OF BARNACLE FEEDING

	Degrees F.	Rate of Feeding per Minute (Four Trials)	Average Rate at Temperature
1)		— , — , — , —	
2)		— , — , — , —	
3)		— , — , — , —	
4)		— , — , — , —	
5)		— , — , — , —	

Location:

Date:

Weather Conditions:

you discover about the relationship between temperature and the rate at which barnacles feed? (See Chapter Note 3 for information on conditions that will affect the rate at which barnacles feed.)

Salinity and Feeding Rate. Find a spot in your area where an inland stream enters a saltwater embayment. Put some of this brackish water (a mix of saltwater and fresh water) into a bucket. Do barnacles feed at the same rate when they are submerged in brackish water as they do when they are covered by seawater?

Other Influences on Feeding Rate. What other factors or stimuli influence the feeding of barnacles? As your barnacles are sweeping the water with their cerri, make a shadow that falls over the water where they are feeding. What happens? How does this behavior protect the barnacles? Grind up some barnacles and mix the material with seawater. With your medicine dropper, place a few drops of this liquid in the water close to the feeding barnacles. What happens? How do you think that this behavior is an advantage to the barnacles?

Succession in a Barnacle Community. Succession is a predictable pattern of change that occurs over time in communities of plants and animals. This important ecological concept applies to the intertidal area, and it is easily observed in the barnacle zone. An investigation of succession along the rocky coast is best carried out between the months of March and June.

Select an area that is about two feet by two feet square. Scrape the rocks clean of all algae, seaweeds, and animals living there. You can outline the clean area with a few dots of colored nail polish. Return to your study area at weekly intervals and record any changes that occur. A chart similar to the one below will be helpful in organizing your findings. Include the name of the area, and note whether it is a zone of high wave energy or tucked among the rocks in the quiet waters of a cove.

What size are the new barnacles? Where did they come from? How did they get there? What kinds of seaweeds are growing there?

What animals and/or seaweeds compete with barnacles for space in your study area?

What a Barnacle Is Made Of. To discover the material that makes up the barnacle cone and its movable plates, place a few drops of acetic acid (vinegar) on the plates. Use your hand lens to observe what happens. (See Chapter Note 4 for additional comments.)

CHAPTER NOTES

1. **Life Zones in the Intertidal Area.** Along the rocky shore, barnacles tend to populate the highest region of the mid-intertidal zone. Below them are rockweeds, followed by mussels. Immediately above the barnacles, in the upper intertidal or black zone, are the rough periwinkles tucked into rock crevices where they are protected from wave action.

SUCCESSION OF ALGAE AND ANIMALS ON A SET OF ROCKS AT MEAN HIGH WATER

Date	Number of Barnacles	Number and Type of Algae or Seaweeds	Number and Type of Other Animals

Location:

Weather Conditions:

Season:

2. Structural Adaptations to Crowding. Barnacles that live where there is plenty of room have a characteristic volcano shape. However, when barnacles are squeezed together, the external shape is elongated so that the individual requires less room on the rock surface. This is a handy adaptation when space is at a premium.

3. Factors That Influence Feeding Rates. There are several other factors that influence barnacle feeding. Certainly the availability of food in the water column is one of the controlling variables. The amount of oxygen in the water is another. Investigating feeding rates can be complicated by these limiting factors.

4. The Acid Test. Vinegar and other acids will form carbon dioxide in the presence of calcium compounds, such as calcium carbonate. When the reaction occurs, you will see vigorous bubbling.

CHAPTER 2

The Sea Star

SURVIVOR AND SYMBOL

Of all marine invertebrates (animals without backbones), sea stars are among the best known. Often used as symbols of the seashore, sea stars are usually one of the first animals that come to mind when we think about life along the rocky coast. There is a good reason for their reputation: these cousins of sand dollars and sea urchins are exclusively marine, never found on land or in fresh water.

Like most predators, sea stars are typically found below the low tide line; they are often discovered flattened against rocks and hidden by curtains of seaweed. They inhabit the large pools formed as the tide recedes along the rocky shore. They thrive in the waters from the Gulf of Maine to Texas and along coastal Alaska to Baja California.

Fossil records tell us that sea stars have been around for a long time. They appeared in the early Cambrian period, about 600 million years ago, and have remained relatively unchanged since then. Although these survivors from the early seas are often called starfish, this is misleading, since they are not fish.

Sea stars belong to a group of animals that scientists call echinoderms. This term comes from two Greek words that mean *hedgehog* and *skin*, so we actually call the members of this group, or phylum, the "spiny-skinned" animals. One of their most obvious characteristics is their radial design; sea stars have five or more sturdy rays extending outward from a flattened central disc. Each of the rays, or arms, contains an extension of the animal's digestive and reproductive systems; therefore the rays are an integral part of the body and not merely appendages.

The internal skeleton of sea stars is made of spine-bearing plates, called ossicles, fashioned from calcium carbonate (chalk). The plates, loosely held

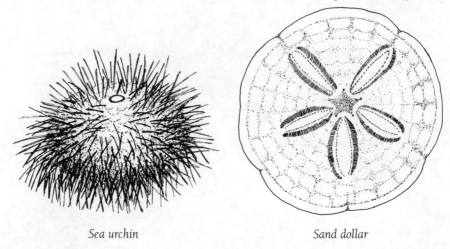

Sea urchin   *Sand dollar*

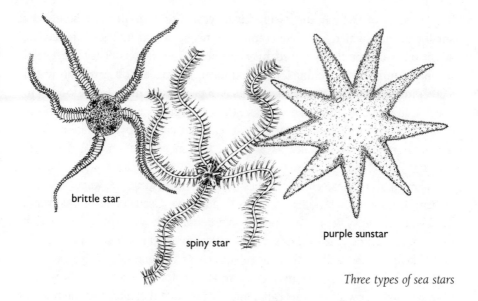

brittle star

spiny star

purple sunstar

Three types of sea stars

together by connective tissue within the animal's delicate skin, give a certain degree of rigidity to the sea star's body. Since the plates are not fused into a single shell, sea stars are remarkably supple. Because they forage in the rough terrain of the intertidal zone, the sea star's ability to bend and twist is essential to its survival.

Since every living thing needs oxygen, one of our first questions about the sea star is, How does it breathe? With the aid of a hand lens, you can see tiny, finger-like extensions of thin skin growing around the base of each spine on the upper surface of the sea star. These are the skin gills through which the animal breathes. Each gill is equipped with beating cilia that create swirling eddies of water. The currents promote the exchange of oxygen and carbon dioxide through the animal's skin.

While examining the skin with your magnifier, look for the tiny pincers, which resemble clam shells perched on flexible stalks. These modified spines keep the slow-moving sea stars from becoming overgrown by barnacles, algae, and other debris that would severely interfere with the functioning of the skin gills. Under the control of the animal's muscular system, these little forceps capture and discard small plants and animals that settle on top of the sea star. To further facilitate housekeeping chores, the sea star secretes an irritating toxin that effectively eliminates those hitchhikers overlooked by the tiny tweezers. All of these mechanisms used by sea stars to keep themselves clean perform extremely well. You'll never see a healthy sea star encrusted by algae or barnacles!

At the tip of each ray, there's a reddish eyespot that can perceive light. Very small tentacles, which look like common pins, surround it. These are feelers, sensitive to chemicals dissolved in water and to vibrations. They are useful when the animal is searching for its next meal. The patient observer can watch a creeping sea star curl the tip of a ray as if to peer in the direction of food or to check out a nearby disturbance. Thus, the tip of each ray functions as an eye that is sensitive to light and dark, as an ear that can receive vibrations from the environment, and finally, as a tongue and nose that serve as chemical receptors.

Though all of these characteristics are very interesting, the water-vascular system, unique to echinoderms, is truly amazing. Used for locomotion and food getting, the system is a series of interconnected, water-filled canals that extends throughout the animal's body. Water enters the sea star through the sieve-like plate located on the upper surface of the animal, called the sieve plate. This colored spot is frequently mistaken for an eye. From here, the seawater flows down the stone canal into a ring canal that encircles the mouth, and then into radial canals, one in each arm. Hundreds of tiny, waving tube feet, which can be seen on the underside of the animal, are connected to the radial canals. In most sea stars, the tube feet end in suckers, which adhere strongly to solid surfaces.

Sea stars can extend and retract each of these thousands of "feet" by forcing seawater in, or drawing it out, of each tube foot. This action also operates a tiny suction cup at the tip of each foot. In order to walk, the sea star must coordinate the extension and retraction process.

As voracious carnivores, sea stars will eat anything they can catch if they

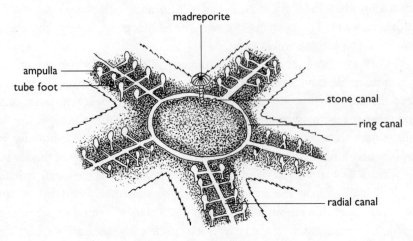

Water-vascular system of a sea star

THE ROCKY SHORE

are very hungry. Otherwise, they will wait for a meal of bivalve mollusks, such as mussels, oysters, or quahogs (clams), which they particularly enjoy. Since they are slow moving animals, most of their prey are sedentary.

Having located a living bivalve, the sea star wraps its strong arms around the shells and positions itself so that two arms are on one side of its meal and three arms are on the other side. The sea star puts its mouth over the seam where the two shells join. Thus positioned, the sea star begins the unrelenting pull to separate the shells that protect the soft body inside.

While the sea star pulls, the mollusk strains to keep its armor clamped together. But, alas, inevitably the clam is overcome by exhaustion. Its shells pop open, and the sea star pushes its stomach out of its body and slips it into the opening between the two shells. Once inside, glands in the stomach secrete digestive enzymes. These powerful chemicals kill the mollusk and reduce it to a soupy liquid, which the sea star stomach absorbs. When the meal is completed, the sea star slowly withdraws its stomach and moves on.

Creeping through the underwater fields of seaweed, these cunning and powerful predators are in control. They're often unbidden visitors to oyster beds, which they have been known to decimate overnight. In some places, they have brought the shellfish industry to its knees. Actually, shellfishermen aided their enemy by chopping the sea stars into pieces, thinking they were killing them. What the shellfishermen did not know was that sea stars can regenerate as long as some of the central disc is attached to the pieces thrown back into the sea. Clearly, these echinoderms called sea stars are successful by any standard of measure, and they did it all without head or brain.

THE WORLD OF THE SEA STAR

What you will need	Science skills
basic kit	*observing*
clear plastic container	*recording*
rough wood	*measuring*
smooth plastic	*comparing*
a piece of sandpaper	
sturdy string	
cotton ball or wool	

OBSERVATIONS

The Anatomy of the Sea Star. Your first task will be to obtain a live sea star. Since sea stars must be completely covered by water to survive, you will need to search in shallow water, in the tide pools, and especially on the sides of

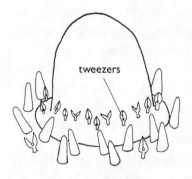

tweezers

Spine projecting from bony lumps (ossides) under a sea star's skin

rocks just under the water's surface. Don't forget to look on pilings and along docks and wharves. After thoroughly wetting your hands in seawater, pick up a sea star and put it, prickly side up, in the palm of your hand. Don't worry, they can't bite or sting. Now, with your other hand, rub your fingers along the back of the sea star. The lumps and bumps you feel on the sea star are part of the animal's skeleton. If you gently pinch the rays, or arms, of your sea star, you can feel the calcium carbonate plates that are part of the framework that gives the animal its formal name, echinoderm. This internal structure also provides protection against predators.

With the sea star in this position you can easily see the radial symmetry that characterizes echinoderms. Animals that illustrate this kind of symmetry are those that can be sectioned like a wagon wheel and have a central disc or hub. Other echinoderms are the sea urchins and the sand dollars.

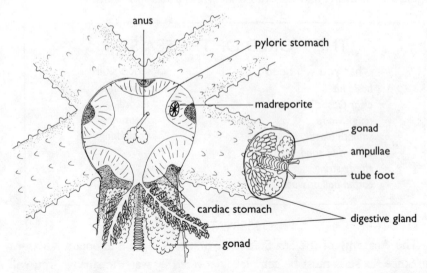

A look inside the sea star

The Eyes of the Sea Star. Use a strong hand lens and look carefully at the tip of each of the five arms. You'll see tiny red dots about the size of pin heads. These are the animal's eyes. Although unable to see objects, sea star eyes are sensitive to light and dark. After you have seen your sea star move, you'll probably be able to explain why the eyes are located on the tips of the rays and not on the animal's "head."

Sea Star Pincers at Work. Place the sea star, prickly side down, on the hairy part of your arm. After a few minutes slowly pull the animal from your arm. Do you feel the tiny pedicellaria, or pincers, at work? If you prefer, you could put a piece of wool or a cotton ball on the prickly side of the sea star. After a few minutes slowly pull the wool or cotton away. What happens?

Put the sea star in a dish and cover it with fresh seawater. Sprinkle some sand grains on the animal's back. What happens to the sand particles? Can you see the tiny pincers at work with your hand lens? Their job, removing debris from the skin and protecting the skin gills, is essential to the well-being of the sea star.

The Sieve Plate. Look at the raised disc near the center of the sea star on the prickly upper surface. (Sometimes it is orange or yellow.) This is the sieve plate, or madreporite. Use your hand lens to see a pattern of small holes that looks like a tea strainer. This disc is a vital part of the sea star's water-vascular system, since seawater is filtered through it and brought into the water-vascular system. If you are observing a variety of species, you have probably noticed that the color of the disc is not always the same. Sieve-plate color is only one of the differences between species of sea stars. How many different species of sea stars can you find? How are the species alike and how are they different? (See Chapter Note 1 for information on different kinds of sea stars.)

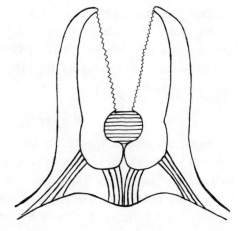

Tweezers-like pedicellaria prevents tiny plants and animals from settling on the sea star.

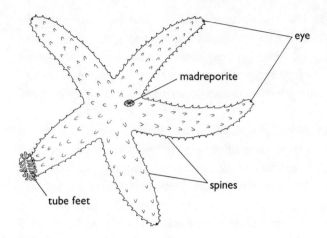

The outside of a sea star

Tube Feet. Turn the sea star over so that the tiny tube feet are visible. How would you describe their motion and position relative to each other? Another way to observe the functioning of the tube feet is to put the sea star on a wet transparent surface so that you can look up at the feet in motion. As the animal moves, watch the tube feet. Is there a pattern to their movement? In your field notebook, write a short description of what you see.

Measuring Sea Star Arms. Wet your hands again with seawater, and put your sea star, prickly side up, in the palm of your hand. How many rays, or arms, does it have? Find out how long each ray is by measuring from the middle of the central disc to the tip of the ray. How long is the longest ray? How short is the shortest? How many of them are short? Do other sea stars of the same species have the same number of short rays? If you can find other types of sea stars, repeat the exercise. What did you find out? How do lengths of rays compare from one species to another?

Squatters on Sea Stars. If you look in the grooves between the tube feet, you may find tiny scale worms living there. How many can you find? Why do you think the worms live with this predator? (See Chapter Note 2 for a brief explanation.)

EXPLORATIONS

Sea Stars on the Move. Try putting the sea star, feet side down, on different surfaces, such as a sturdy piece of smooth plastic, a rough board, or a large piece of sandpaper. These materials should be large enough to provide room for the sea star to move about without falling off. How do these different surfaces affect the manner of movement and the time it takes the sea star to go from one place to another? Does the sea star always lead with the same arm? What do you think determines which arm the sea star will use first?

Put a stone in the path of a moving sea star. What does the animal do when it touches the object? Place different objects in its path. What happens? Put a small piece of chicken or dead fish in the path of the sea star. What does the sea star do?

The Sea Star Somersault. On a firm surface, place a sea star feet side up, and observe the animal as it turns over. Write a description in your field notebook of how the sea star does this little trick. How long does it take to turn itself over? Does the size of the sea star affect the speed of turnover? What is the role of the tube feet in the somersault? Try the same thing in wet sand. Watch for the tips of the rays to dig into the sand as they aid in the turnover process. Do different species of sea stars turn over in the same way?

What Causes a Sea Star to Turn Over? You have seen how a sea star turns itself right side up, but how does the animal *know* that it is upside down? Researchers believe that the series of actions that turns a sea star over is stimulated when the tube feet are not touching a surface. You can test this idea by making a cradle out of sturdy thread and suspending the sea star, feet side up. What happens? Now suspend the sea star in a cradle while its feet are toward the ground but still not touching any surface. What happens?

A Gourmet Delight. With patience and some good luck, you might get to observe a sea star feeding. You could encourage this process by placing some pieces of oysters or mussels in a container of seawater with a sea star. Add a live clam or mussel that's still in its shell. To keep the system going for an extended period, you might have to aerate the water with a fish tank pump. With a bit of luck, you will see the sea star evert its stomach, digest its meal, and "drink" the nutritious liquid. How long does the process take? Write the sequence of steps that you observe in this process.

CHAPTER NOTES

1. **Different Kinds of Sea Stars.** *Asterias* species are very common sea stars from Penobscot Bay, Maine, to the Gulf of Mexico. There are two species, which resemble each other except for the color of the madreporite. In species *Asterias forbessi*, it is usually orange, while in the species *Asterias vulgaris*, it is usually yellow. Blood stars are found from the Arctic to Cape Hatteras, North Carolina, while the slender sea star haunts the waters from Cape Hatteras, North Carolina, to Brazil, South America. Species of sunstars (having more than five arms) are found from the Arctic to Cape Cod. West coast cousins that belong to the sea star group called Asteroidea are the ochre sea star (*Pisaster*

ochraceus) and the giant sea star (*Pisaster gigantium*). The ochre sea star begins its range as far north as Alaska. It joins the giant sea star at British Columbia, and they both roam the waters all the way to Baja California. See one of the field guides suggested in the bibliography for further information.

2. Squatters. The presence of the scale worms doesn't harm the sea star. The worms probably benefit from the relationship, since they probably eat the bits of food scraps that result from the sea star's meal. This symbiotic relationship, called commensalism, is common among animals that live in intertidal habitats, and the relationship accounts for a substantial amount of nutrient recycling and energy flow in food webs.

CHAPTER 3

The Slipper Limpet

TOTEM POLE MOLLUSK

Along the rocky coast, life stories are being woven by countless numbers of plants and animals. Each organism tells its own tale with a rhythm that is as metered as the beat of a metronome. These vignettes, regularly told, will be shared with the beach stroller who takes a little time to linger, look, and listen. Once such yarn is woven by animals called slipper limpets. Since their shells are not very pretty by commercial standards, they tend to be ignored by the casual beachcomber.

Their common name, slipper shell, comes from the pocket found on the underside of the shell. This pocket, or shelf, keeps the digestive organs of the animal in place. Empty slipper shells can be found along the beach and are generally mixed with the debris that has been tossed ashore by wave action.

If you wander among the slippery rocks and seaweed at low tide, you may find, on the smooth surface of a rock, a small stack of beige-colored shells arranged by size. The largest of the shells, perhaps somewhat smaller than the bowl of a teaspoon, is at the bottom of the stack. If you discover this mollusk along the beaches of the Atlantic rocky shore, you have found the common Atlantic slipper shell, or *Crepidula fornucata*. This east coast mollusk can also be found on the beaches of Washington State where it has been introduced. Another stacking, or totem pole, mollusk fills a similar niche south of Monterey, California. This is the onyx slipper shell, *Crepidula onyx*. Both types of slipper shell animals change sex as they grow, so the larger female is on the bottom, while the smaller males reside toward the top of the stack.

Along the Atlantic shores, you might also come across another, but less common, slipper limpet, *Crepidula plana*, or lady's slipper shell. This limpet does not form stacks and has a whitish shell. You can often find this limpet on

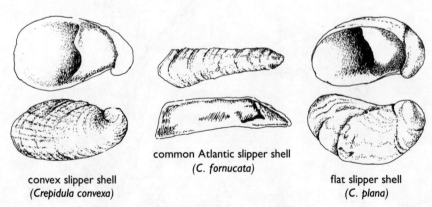

convex slipper shell
(*Crepidula convexa*)

common Atlantic slipper shell
(*C. fornucata*)

flat slipper shell
(*C. plana*)

Three types of slipper limpets

the underside of the exoskeleton of horseshoe crabs. The lady's slipper also sets up housekeeping inside the discarded shells of whelks and large moon snails. Another tribe of slipper limpets is *Crepidula convexa*, or the convex slipper shell. These, like their cousins *C. plana* and *C. fornucata*, are found from the Gulf of Mexico to Massachusetts and scattered locally in the Gulf of St. Lawrence. The spiny slipper limpet, *Crepidula aculeata*, makes its home along the Atlantic from North Carolina to Texas and in the shallows south of central California.

Slipper limpets, a type of snail, belong to a large phylum of animals called mollusks. Like others in this phylum, they lack internal structural stiffeners, such as bones and a spinal cord. Snails are their close cousins.

The slipper limpet lives in the intertidal zone, where it's securely anchored to rock surfaces by the strong sucking action of its muscular foot. Since it is a vegetarian, after a brief period of wandering while young, the slipper limpet takes up permanent residence wherever the seawater contains plenty of microscopic plant material.

Although related to snails, the slipper limpet lacks the rasping, tongue-like radula that its cousins use to scrape food from rock surfaces. Instead, slipper limpets have enlarged gills that are covered with tiny, hair-like projections, called cilia. The constant beating of the cilia causes eddies in the surrounding water, which flows in around the edges of the shell. This swirling water passes by the top of the animal's foot, which is covered by a sticky substance. Nutrients suspended in the water are trapped by this mucus and stored there until the animal needs them.

The slipper limpet illustrates a distinctly different way of eating. Every four minutes or so, it twists its mouth from one side to the other, gathering in the mucus with its supply of food. The smaller morsels are eaten right away, while the larger pieces are stored in a pouch at the front of the animal's mouth. While many animals eat all the food that's available at any given time, the slipper limpet eats only what it needs. Therefore, the leftovers are stored in the pouch and become emergency rations, which are used during periods of drought, such as low tide.

Since each meal is brought to slipper limpets in the tidal water, there's no need for them to move from place to place the way their grazing relatives, the snails, must do. Therefore, once settled, *Crepidula* remain firmly attached!

Frequently, *Crepidula fornucata* is found attached to rocks along the shore. More often, however, you will find them attached to other mollusks, especially to each other. In this latter arrangement, they form neat stacks that contain seven to thirteen individuals, although the usual number is ten.

These unit stacks illustrate the life cycle of the common Atlantic slipper limpet, *Crepidula fornucata* and *Crepidula onyx*. The stack contains successive generations in which each individual in the series is one year younger than the animal to which it is attached. The individuals in this gastropod totem pole have a curious relationship to each other. The smallest, and sexually immature, males are at the top of the stack. The next three down, somewhat larger, are mature males. These are followed by two bisexual, or transitional, males, and finally, two large mature females. The bottom member of the pile is usually attached to a dead shell. Thus slipper limpets are quite logically called sequential hermaphrodites. This means that they begin life as males, develop into bisexuals, and finally become females in the later stages of their lives. Those who enjoy playing with words might like to know that an organism with this life-style is called, in more formal circles, a protandric hermaphrodite.

Such a reproductive arrangement functions very efficiently, since the males at the top fertilize the bisexual individuals below, and they in turn fertilize each other as well as the females at the bottom of the stack. This behavior illustrates another reason for the animals' stationary existence.

Although the Atlantic slipper limpet and the onyx slipper limpet change sex as they mature, the timing of these changes is influenced by several factors, including water temperature and the type of food that's available. In addition, the females release a chemical scent (pheromone) into the water that is responsible for keeping the males male! When the males live in isolation, they become females sooner than is good for the survival of the species.

The east coast *Crepidula* take great care of their spawn. Each fertilized adult makes about forty-five sacs from a membranous material. It then puts about 250 fertilized eggs into each sac. The sacs are secured with a cord. The cord then gets attached to the rock where the adult is located. Thus, the eggs are protected for about a month until they hatch. This kind of protection is extremely rare in those organisms we flippantly call "lower animals."

When hatched, the newly developed larvae leave the adult commune to

Male slipper limpet at the top fertilizes the bisexual below

THE ROCKY SHORE

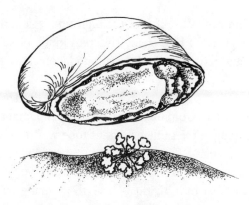

Female slipper limpet and egg sacs

fend for themselves among the free-swimming plankton. Of the thousands of larvae that emerge, relatively few will live to join existing slipper-limpet communities and begin their journey through sexual transformation.

THE WORLD OF THE SLIPPER LIMPET

What you will need
basic kit
colored nail polish
patience

Science skills
observing
measuring
recording

OBSERVATIONS

Finding Slipper Limpets. Although there are several types of slipper limpets, probably the first kind you'll notice will be those that are attached to each other in small stacks. These are the common slipper limpets (*Crepidula fornucata*) or onyx slipper limpets (*Crepidula onyx*). You may also find other types of slipper shells, such as the convex slipper shell (*Crepidula convexa*) and lady's slipper shell (*Crepidula plana*). To locate slipper limpets, carefully lift the seaweed curtains that cover the rocks, and explore the cracks and crevices of the rocky coast at low tide. Also examine the shells of clams, whelks, moon snails, and mussels, and the sheds of horseshoe crabs scattered throughout the intertidal zone. Don't forget to look at old soda bottles and the like.

Identifying the Slipper Shells. With the help of your field guide or the illustration on page 32, identify the slipper limpet that you found. Did you find the common slipper shell, the convex slipper shell, or the lady's slipper shell? Perhaps you found the spiny slipper limpet. Try to find all four types, and write a description of them or draw pictures of them in your notebook. Include information in your notes about the habitat of the limpets that you found. At what level of the intertidal zone did you find the different types of slipper limpets? Were they at the high-tide region, the mid-tide region, or the low-tide region? To how many different kinds of substrates or foundations were they attached? What did these foundations have in common?

EXPLORATIONS

The Community of the Slipper Limpet. Slipper limpets are often found living in the same habitat as tube worms, chitons, flatworms, brittle stars, and sea slugs. What animals did you find living in the same habitat as your slipper limpets? Make a list of the animals you find and include the approximate number of individuals in each animal group. Which of them occurred most frequently? Least frequently?

Stacks of Slipper Limpets. Find some stacks of the common slipper limpet (*Crepidula fornucata*) or the onyx slipper limpet (*Crepidula onyx*). How many individuals do you find in each stack? What is the largest number of individuals living together? What was the smallest number of individuals in a stack? Where did you find these stacks? Measure the length of the individuals in each stack. Compare the differences in length of successive individuals in different stacks. Keep this information, since it may relate to local pollution conditions.

Movement of Slipper Limpets. Since slipper limpets are attached to a rock by suction, rather than being glued in place like barnacles, some people have thought that they move about. This is an idea that can be investigated. Find a stack of slipper limpets and mark the rock close to them with a small amount of colored nail polish. Observe the stack over a period of several days. If you

SOME OF THE OTHER CREATURES IN A SLIPPER-LIMPET COMMUNITY—A SURVEY

Animals	Total Number	Animals	Total Number
a. tube worms		g. drill snails	
b. chitons		h. isopods	
c. flatworms		i. amphipods	
d. sea stars		j. urchins	
e. sea slugs		k. others	
f. crabs			

Location:

Date:

Weather Conditions:

can, find more than one of these stacks to watch. Try to go back every few hours during the first day and then once or twice every day for the next few days. What is your conclusion? Do slipper limpets move? Try gently to remove a slipper limpet from its foundation or substrate. Would you say that the attachment is firm enough to resist wave action? What other survival advantage is this kind of attachment for the slipper limpet?

Pollution and Limpet Growth Rates. During the spring, the immature *Crepidula* grow an average of six millimeters in three weeks. Particulate pollution, which doesn't dissolve in the water, is not strained through the limpet's gill system. Instead, it clogs the system and reduces the amount of nutrients that can be absorbed by the limpet. Consequently, the growth rate is slowed. If you have sufficient inclination and patience, you can use your records of limpet length to keep track of the growth of a few limpets for a period of time. This information can be very useful in measuring the effects of various kinds of pollution.

CHAPTER 4

The
Blue Mussel

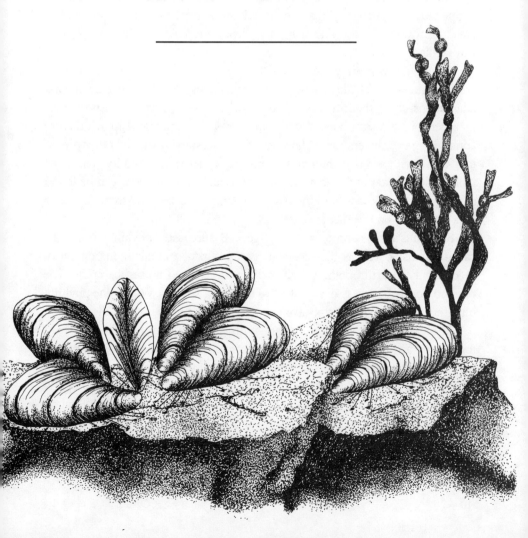

Imperceptibly, the tide ebbs and slowly exposes the thin strip of land that belongs alternately to the land and then to the sea. The rocky shore gleams from the wetness left by the retreating water. Rocky ledges, festooned with seaweed, begin to appear, then large boulders encrusted with bands of white are seen, and finally, after a while, black bands gradually emerge. These exposed bands of life contain populations of barnacles, *Fucus* (rockweed), mussels, and other life forms, which compete for food and space in the intertidal zone. If you stand near these exposed communities, you can hear fizzing, hissing, crackling sounds as they carry on the routine business of life.

Since this region is rhythmically flooded and drained every six hours or so, the creatures that make their living here have developed unusual adaptations to deal with the rigors of prolonged exposure to water and wind. Additionally, they have strategies that help them adjust to extreme and rapid changes in temperature, to changes in salinity, to winter storms, to scouring ice, and to crashing waves. For the organisms that live here, environmental stress is a way of life.

Among the vast array of animals that cope with the rigors of this habitat are blue mussels (*Mytilus edulis*). Their marvelous structural and behavioral adaptations allow them to flourish and to become, at least for a short time, members of the rocky shore climax community. This membership in a mature community is only temporary, however, since sea stars, man, and other predators will alter their distribution and numbers in the community. Thus, the biological character of the area changes continually. Blue mussels can be found along the Atlantic coast from the Arctic to South Carolina, and from Alaska to Baja California on the Pacific coast.

Blue mussels belong to a very large and successful phylum of animals called mollusks. This is the second largest group of animals living on earth, second only to arthropods, which include insects and horseshoe crabs. The phylum boasts in excess of seventy-five thousand species. Within the phylum, blue mussels belong to the bivalve class because they have two shells.

The two-shelled animals, hinged with a gristle-like ligament, are held together by a strong abductor, or closing muscle. These calcareous shells can be tightly closed to shield the soft-bodied animal inside from a pounding surf, which is often armed with rocks, logs, or chunks of ice. Additionally, a tightly closed shell offers protection from the heat of day and prevents the infiltration of fresh water from a heavy rainfall.

The shells are manufactured by the mantle. This outermost layer of the animal's body lines the inner surface of the shell and is the primary organ of respiration. Additionally, the mantle manufactures calcium, thus producing successive layers of shell. Each layer projects a little beyond the last layer laid down, adding to the shell's thickness and length. The age of a mussel can be determined by counting the number of wide, concentric bands that appear on the handsome blue-black shell.

Another survival strategy that has developed in blue mussels is the production of an enormous number of tiny eggs. One female can manufacture ten to twenty million eggs in a single breeding season. The development and subsequent release of these microscopic eggs is triggered by a very slight increase in water temperature that occurs sometime in late winter or early spring. Furthermore, chemicals discharged into the sea at this time by spawning individuals stimulate egg production in other female mussels, as well as the release into the water of a tremendous number of sperm by male mussels. These gametes fuse and form larvae, which show no resemblance to adult mussels. The larvae are swept to new locations by water currents, thus ensuring a broad distribution of new mussel populations. Although these methods of reproduction and distribution of mussels from one place to another seem haphazard, undeniably they work.

Like the young of many other marine invertebrates, mussel larvae spend their early days as drifters in the plankton community. They develop rapidly, and the larval mussels that escape predation settle to the bottom, where they metamorphose into their adult form. Using their agile, finger-like, muscular foot to touch and test, the tiny mussels probe along the bottom in search of a suitable place to settle.

Answering the chemical signals sent out by the adult population, the young mussels snuggle into the tiny spaces between individuals in the already densely packed mussel beds. In this way, the young extend the length and width of the living bivalve blanket that covers the rocks of the intertidal zone.

In an adult mussel, the muscular foot becomes too flabby to be of any use in locomotion. Instead, it houses the byssal gland, which secretes strong protein strings that harden in the water. When the probing foot touches a desirable object like a rock, piling, or even other mussels, it releases a drop of byssus secretion. When this material hits a solid surface, it forms the disc of attachment. When the animal withdraws its foot, the first thread of the anchor line system is formed. This process is repeated until there are enough threads to firmly hold the animal to the choice spot.

Should food or space be in short supply, mussels can release some of their mooring lines, reel in others, and move to a more desirable location at the rate of a foot or so per day.

Mussels are filter feeders. This means that they draw currents of water, rich in food and oxygen, into their mantle cavity through an "incoming" siphon. The water is then pulled through tiny pores in the sieve-like gills, leaving suspended food particles, sand, and other debris on the gill surface. The gills, or food collecting organs, are covered with tiny hairs called cilia. The cilia vary in size and have different functions. For example, some cilia sort the particles that have been left on the gill surface. Still others mix the food with mucus and carry this food package to the mouth. The cilia discharge waste materials into the water currents, so that they can be excreted through the "outgoing" siphon.

Because of their feeding method, blue mussels are collectors and accumulators of toxic materials, such as nitrates and bacteria. Although these materials don't appear to harm the mussel, they can be extremely dangerous to any of us that eat mussels from polluted waters. On the other hand, we can look upon these filter feeders as allies in our struggle against pollution, since each mussel filters about twenty-five gallons of water per day. With up to a million mussels to the acre in some shore areas, this filtration process is an important part of nature's water purification program.

THE WORLD OF THE BLUE MUSSEL

What you will need
basic kit
string
hand-held spring scale
food coloring
shallow pan

Science skills
observing
recording
measuring

OBSERVATIONS

Where to Find Blue Mussels. Look for blue mussels at low tide along the rocky shore where they compete with seaweeds and barnacles for space and food. At what level in the intertidal zone did you find them? Are they living at the level of high tide, mid-tide, or low tide? In what other places do you find them? Be sure to examine pilings and jetties. Where on these structures do you find mussels relative to other animals living there?

How the Mussels Attach Themselves. As you were hunting for mussels, you probably noticed that they adhere to a variety of objects by a system of strings or byssal threads. Make a list of the different objects that you found mussels attached to. Which foundations are most often used by mussels? What do these objects have in common? (See Chapter Note 1 for an explanation.)

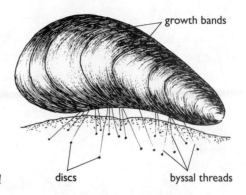

growth bands

The outside of the blue mussel   discs   byssal threads

The byssal threads, or "beards," are one of the most familiar characteristics of blue mussels. Spun by a gland in the animal's foot, the threads serve to anchor the mussels to rocks, to pilings, and even to other stationary animals. Look for the tiny disc at the end of each thread; use a hand lens to examine the disc. With the help of some very strong glue produced by the mussels, the discs hold the mussels firmly in place.

Hold one or two of the byssal threads between your thumb and forefinger. Tug on them. Are they brittle? Are they elastic?

The Relationship between Threads and the Size of the Mussel. Often it looks as though mussels are attached to rocks and other objects by a tangle of byssal threads. Is there a relationship between the number of threads from mussels and the size of the object to which they are attached? Is there a relationship between the length of the mussel and the number of threads it spins?

Mussel Shape and Orientation. Mussels survive in a rigorous environ-

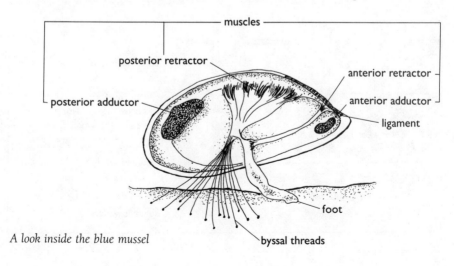

muscles

posterior retractor

anterior retractor

posterior adductor

anterior adductor

ligament

A look inside the blue mussel

foot

byssal threads

ment; they are often exposed to storm waves and strong currents. They have adapted to this habitat in a variety of ways. Examine various groups of mussels. How are they positioned in the clumps? Is the pointed end facing up or is it facing down? Do they all seem to be facing in the same direction? Do you think this orientation provides an advantage? What is the shape of the shell? How is this shape an advantage over the more rectangular shape of clams that burrow in the mud? (See Chapter Note 2 for a discussion of the shape of mussels.)

EXPLORATIONS

Succession on a Submerged Object. You have seen that many marine algae and animals make their permanent homes on pilings. In the spring, when mussel larvae are among the many animals adrift in the plankton community, you can discover a sequence of events that leads to an established piling community. To do this exploration, you need something about four feet long that sinks and that has holes for a rope on one end. You can use a length of old metal pipe or a length of plastic pipe (PVC), two inches or so in diameter, or a wooden two-by-four with a weight screwed to the bottom end. You will need access to a dock or bulkhead where you can dangle your "piling" on a rope so that it is just underwater at high tide. Tie the free end of the rope to the dock where it will not interfere with dockside traffic. Leave the plank for about two months, checking it about once a week for any signs that animals or algae (seaweeds) are growing on it.

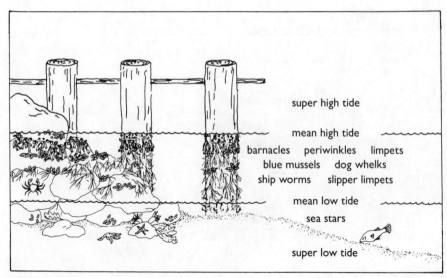

Intertidal zonation

How long did it take for a thin film of algae to develop on the "piling"? The first set of observations is to note the sequence of life over time. Which animal or other seaweed follows the algae? The second set of observations is to note the vertical sequence of developing life. What life forms finally develop at the top, farther down, and at the bottom? Keep a careful record of your observations. A chart would be helpful: draw the object and indicate on the drawing the animals and algae as they occur.

At the end of your experiment, summarize what you found out about the time sequence and the vertical sequence in which marine life developed on your submerged object. Try the experiment again in other parts of the intertidal zone on the rocky shore. Do you find a similar sequence of events?

The Age of a Mussel. As mussels grow, the mantel produces calcium and deposits this new calcium at the wide end of both halves of the shell. The annual growth of each mussel is indicated by the width of the distinct, wide bands that you see on the outside of the shell. Find a bunch of mussels and measure the width of the last band formed. How much did each of them grow in that year? By counting the number of wide bands, the age of mussels can be determined, although it's difficult to distinguish the bands close to the pointed end. What is the approximate age of some mussels you found?

Many factors determine how much a mussel will grow in a given year. One of these determinants is the amount of food available in the water. Another factor affecting growth is the amount of time available for feeding. Since mussels are filter feeders, is there a relationship between their location in the intertidal zone and the total amount of growth? Which ones have the most time to feed? Are the mussels that live high in the intertidal zone (group A) smaller than those that live low in the intertidal zone (group B)? Find an equal number of mussels in each zone (perhaps a dozen), and measure the length of each one. What is the average length for each group? A chart similar to the one below will help you organize your information.

Observing the Siphons. To find the position of the siphons in your mussels, fill a shallow pan with seawater, and submerge the mussels. How long does it take the animal to relax its abductor muscle and open its shell? A siphon is a small tube that a mollusk uses to move water in or out. What differences do you see between the two siphons? Is there a relationship between the diameter of the siphons and the length of the mussels?

Through which siphon does the mussel draw in nutrient-rich water? (Which siphon is the incurrent siphon?) And through which siphon does the animal expel water? (Which siphon is the excurrent siphon?) Although you can usually see a turbulence near a siphon as water is expelled from it, try

POSITION IN THE INTERTIDAL ZONE AND
GROWTH RATE OF BLUE MUSSELS

Group A—High Intertidal Zone		Group B—Low Intertidal Zone	
Individual	Length	Individual	Length
1		1	
2		2	
3		3	
4		4	
5		5	
6		6	
7		7	
8		8	
9		9	
10		10	
11		11	
12		12	

Average length _____   **Average length** _____

adding a tiny drop of food coloring very near the ingoing siphon to dramatize the currents. (See Chapter Note 3 for some tips.)

Measuring the Strength of Byssal Threads. Byssal threads are quite strong. To find out how much weight the threads will hold, find a mussel that is attached by a few byssal threads to a small stone. Use a loop of string to attach this stone to the hook of a spring balance with the mussel hanging down supported by its threads. Record its weight. Use Play-Doh or modeling clay to make several small balls of equal size. Stick the balls of clay, one at a time, to

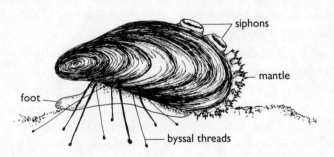

Blue mussel with siphons extended

the mussel shell and record the total weight. How much weight will the threads hold before breaking?

The Mussel Community. Although mussels appear to dominate sections of the intertidal zone, many other organisms live in the community as well. Mark off an area where you have found a population of mussels. Make a list of the other living things that you find among the mussel population. Classify the animals on your list in some way; for example, animals that move from one place to another in search of food and those that do not. Do any of the animals you found prey on the mussels?

CHAPTER NOTES

1. Function of Byssal Threads. Mussels use their byssal threads to attach themselves firmly to something solid that will not be moved by tidal action, storm surge, or wave motion. Thus, mussels will be found attached to rocks, pilings, and other unmovable objects, rather than to seaweed fronds, sand, or mud.

2. Adaptations of Mussel Shells. The shape of mussel shells is an advantageous adaptation for living in the intertidal zone. The shape helps to dissipate or scatter the energy released by waves in a pounding surf. A rectangular shell would not be as effective.

3. The Use of Food Coloring. Place a tiny amount of food coloring in the water very close to the incurrent siphon. You may be able to see some of the colored water enter the intake siphon. If you're lucky, you will see the colored water expelled from the excurrent siphon. You'll have to experiment to determine the right amount of food coloring to use in order to satisfy yourself that you actually saw water movement.

CHAPTER 5

Seaweeds

ROCKY ALGAE GARDENS

Explorers of the rocky shore know that, as the tide recedes, horizontal bands are slowly laid bare across the rocks in the thin strip of earth shared by land and sea. The color of the bands is produced, for the most part, by the green, brown, and red seaweeds that live and flourish there. Higher on the rocks, in the spray zone, large colonies of blue-green algae paint an almost black band, which is often mistaken for pollution from an oil spill.

The seemingly fragile seaweeds often astonish the careful observer with their remarkable diversity. Scientists call seaweeds primitive plants, because they lack leaves, roots, stems, and other specialized structures found in seed-bearing plants, such as trees and grasses. Because seaweeds possess a different set of special features, they have prospered in their watery habitat for the past 500 million years.

Since nutrient-rich waters almost continuously bathe the entire plant, seaweeds don't need roots to absorb water and minerals. Their root-like structures, called holdfasts, have a different role. Although holdfasts come in different forms, all of them use similar methods to hold a seaweed to a firm surface. At the end of each holdfast is a tiny disc that secretes a powerfully strong glue. This substance grips rock surfaces so firmly that only the force of grinding ice and battering storm waves can successfully wrench the plants free. If you have ever tried to pull a seaweed from its point of attachment, you have discovered the effectiveness of this anchoring glue.

A simple blade or a series of branching fronds arises from the holdfast. These are similar in function to the leaves of the more advanced seed plants. The fronds and blades are the photosynthesizing, or food-producing, structures of the seaweeds. Chlorophyll, the green pigment in the fronds, captures solar energy and uses it to convert raw materials into starches and sugars (carbohydrates).

The stems of seed plants contain a system of tubes, called vessels, that transport raw materials and nutrients up from the roots and sugars down from the leaves and stems. But seaweeds don't need such structures. One seaweed, kelp (Laminaria), has ducts that are used for internal transport. Because many seaweeds spend much of their time floating on the surface of the water, they don't need a rigid stem to lift them toward the sun.

While beachcombing, you have probably noticed that some brown seaweeds have a system of gas-filled floats. These bladders serve to keep the plants upright in the water or floating on the surface of the water, maximizing the weeds' exposure to sunlight. This system of floats is almost like a weak-stemmed land plant's sending up a helium balloon to hold itself up.

Children often delight in popping the jelly-bean-sized floats of the two most common seaweeds along the New England coast—knotted wrack, or oarweeds (*Ascophyllum nodosum*), and rockweed (*Fucus*). The smooth air bladders of these seaweeds are sometimes confused with the nubby sacs at the tips of *Fucus*. The nubby sacs contain gametes, or sex cells, which function in the reproductive portion of the seaweed's life cycle.

Some seaweeds have a tough, flexible area between the blade and the holdfast that looks like a stem. This is the stipe, which serves as an effective shock absorber that yields to the push and pull of the currents and waves. You can observe the stipe in action by looking at a bed of kelp (*Laminaria*) along the rocky shore as tidal currents swirl around the supple weeds.

During the course of a tidal cycle, intertidal seaweeds are exposed to the drying effects of summer sun and winter winds. To protect against the constant danger of dehydration, seaweed blades produce a shiny, gelatinous material that minimizes water loss. Anyone who has walked on rocks festooned with seaweeds has had firsthand experience with this slippery moisture guard.

When the tide begins to retreat toward the sea, we hardly notice the first green seaweeds that appear. Among these are sea lettuce (*Ulva*), its light green blades looking good enough to eat, and gut weed (*Enteromorpha*) with its small, hollow green tubes. Strands of this bright green seaweed can be found easily as it lies prostrate on the rocks and boulders that stud the beach profile.

As the tide continues to drop, rockweeds are uncovered. Their colors, ranging from yellow to brown and black, are due to the pigments that mask the bright green of chlorophyll. Finally, and only at the lowest of the low tides, the red weeds appear. Their exposure is so brief that the casual observer rarely sees the deep reds of Irish moss (*Chondrus crispus*) and its relative *Gigartina*, or the delicate crusty branches of *Corallina*, except when they have been ripped from their attachment by violent wave action and thrown onto the beach. (See Chapter Note 1 for a little more information on these red seaweeds.)

The variety of shapes and hues found in red algae is further illustrated by the pink to deep red, flat sheets of *Porphyra*, the delicate branching tufts of *Polysiphonia*, and the antler-like branches of *Gracilaria*. A field guide to the seashore (see suggested guides in the Bibliography) will help you sort out what is often a confusing display of colors and shapes.

People who live on the East Coast often say, "They do things differently on the West Coast." Well, this is true when it comes to seaweeds. When the tide drops on the Pacific side of the continent, red weeds, such as certain species of

Gigartina living in the high-tide region, are among the first to be exposed. Species of *Fucus* appear next; they are followed by *Ulva*, which lives in the mid- to low-tide zone. (For more information, see Carefoot in the Bibliography.)

The horizontal colored bands formed by groups of seaweeds along the intertidal zone is not accidental. They are the result of millions of years of the evolution of photosynthetic pigments. The green weeds, which are uncovered most of the time, contain green chlorophyll chemicals. The brown and red seaweeds also contain chlorophyll, but it is masked by other brown, yellow-orange, and red pigments. These accessory pigments, or "helpers," make it possible for photosynthesis to occur in deep water where light energy is greatly diminished. Scientists have found that some seaweeds flourish at great depths where the intensity of sunlight is barely equivalent to the light of the moon.

As an explorer of the intertidal zone, you have encountered a great variety of those plants that scientists call algae. Most people lump them into one vague group, seaweeds, but now you may know some of them more intimately. As you stand and watch these plants swaying in the waves, you may realize that you are just glimpsing the edges of a great forest. You are looking at the canopy of a hidden world. The discoveries still to be made in this world may prove to be more important to mankind than all other explorations.

THE WORLD OF SEAWEEDS

What you will need
basic kit
plastic container
tweezers
cooler
small plastic bags
kitchen scale
paper towels
cooler
sketch pad
aluminum foil
jars
determination

Science skills
observing
comparing
measuring
inferring
graphing

OBSERVATIONS

Although most seaweeds don't have popular names, you will find that with practice, their scientific names will become easy to say and remember. The little dictionary listed in the Bibliography will help with the Greek and Latin derivations of seaweed names. When you become familiar with these, they will add to the excitement of your discoveries.

Beginning to Observe Seaweeds. A good way to begin observing seaweeds is to find some attached to a small rock or mollusk shell. Although you can find loose strands of seaweed washed up on the beach, the following activities are centered on whole, living seaweeds that you will find at low tide growing in their natural habitat. With the help of the diagram below, you will be able to identify the three main parts of your sample of seaweed. Notice the comparison to the parts of a familiar land plant. How are these parts similar and how do they differ? (See Chapter Note 2 for a discussion of differences between seaweeds and land plants.)

The Holdfast Community. With the help of your hand lens, examine the stipe, blade, and holdfasts. Are there living things present on your seaweed? With the help of your guide book, see if you can find out what they are.

Zones within the Intertidal Area. Tidal flow is the primary nonliving factor that influences the formation of intertidal zones, each of which is distinguished by its own populations of plants and animals. Another nonliving

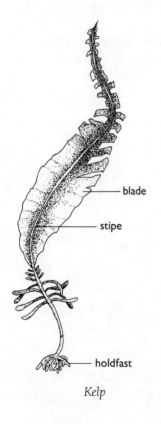

Kelp

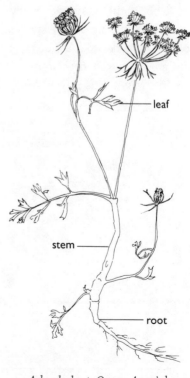

A land plant, Queen Anne's lace

consideration is the particular set of conditions that seaweeds are exposed to, including wave action, variations in the intensity of light, fluctuations in salinity and temperature, and the type of surface available for the holdfasts. (See Chapter Note 3 for some examples of interactions between *living* things that determine zonation in specific coastal areas.)

With the aid of the profile below, determine the zone in which you found your seaweed. Was it in the littoral fringe (the spray zone) or in the mid-littoral zone? (See Chapter Note 4 for a diagram of the zones.)

A Seaweed Collection. Collect about six different types of seaweeds and wrap them in cool, moist paper toweling. You can easily transport your collection in a cooler to a place where you can examine them at your leisure. If it will be some time before you can study them, put the wrapped seaweeds in the refrigerator. As you collect them, record at what level of the intertidal zone you found each species. Was it attached to a rock, a shell, or another object, or was it floating freely in the water?

Comparisons between Seaweeds. How does each different species smell? What color is each of your specimens? Brown, green, olive, pink, purplish red, or some other color? Which color is most common? How does each feel? Soft and flabby? Stiff? Rubbery? Fuzzy? Leathery?

What is the shape of each type? Does the thallus, or body, of the seaweed branch? Is it flat like a leaf or string-like? Is it tubular? Is it thick or thin? Observe the edges, or margins, of the blades of each type of seaweed. Is the margin straight or is it wavy? Is it smooth or toothed?

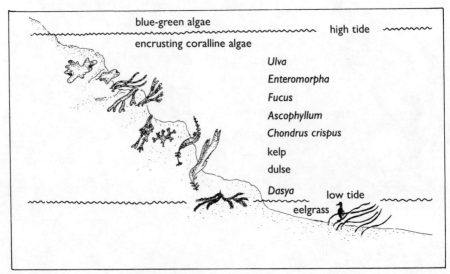

Location of seaweeds in the intertidal zone

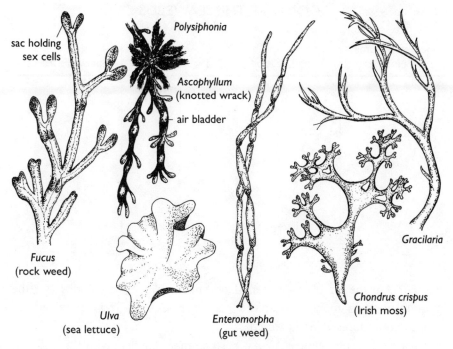

sac holding
sex cells

Polysiphonia

Ascophyllum
(knotted wrack)

— air bladder

Gracilaria

Fucus
(rock weed)

Chondrus crispus
(Irish moss)

Ulva
(sea lettuce)

Enteromorpha
(gut weed)

Some common seaweeds

You can use a chart similar to the one below to organize your observations. If you don't know the name of the seaweed you've collected, simply give the specimen a number and write the corresponding number on your chart.

Drawings of Your Seaweeds. Make a drawing of each specimen and label your drawing with the name of the species. This will help you learn the name of the seaweed and remember some of the characteristics that distinguish it from other species.

The Fucoid Cousins. With the help of your field guide, determine whether you have collected *Fucus spiralis*, *Ascophyllum nodosum*, or *Fucus vesiculosus*.

Where in the intertidal zone did you find these seaweeds relative to each other? Which was found highest in the mid-littoral zone? Which of the three seaweeds did you find midway in the mid-littoral zone? Which one of them did you find lowest in the mid-littoral zone? Only two of these types of seaweeds have air bladders. Do you think this fact is related to the level in the intertidal area in which they grow? (See Chapter Note 5 for a brief explanation of photosynthetic adaptations.)

There are several varieties of *Fucus*, and you probably will not find them in the same vicinity. However, if you vacation in different coastal areas, look for these different varieties. When you find one, ask: Are the blades flat or

COMPARE THE SEAWEEDS

Seaweed Name or Number	Zone Location	Shape	Color	Special Features

twisted? Are the air bladders paired on either side of the midrib? Are the reproductive tips round and soft? Or are they elongated? Keep records of where you find the different varieties.

Seaweed Communities. As you become more familiar with the different types of seaweeds, look for the various animals that live in the same locations as the weeds. Make a list of these creatures and see if you can discover how the seaweeds contribute to their survival.

Springtime along the Rocky Shore. *Fucus:* In the spring you will observe that the tips of *Fucus* blades are swollen and bumpy. These sacs contain male and female gametes, or sex cells. When mature, the gametes are released into the surrounding water. They fuse and develop into new weeds.

Ascophyllum: Look for numerous sacs scattered throughout the length of *Ascophyllum.* These sacs hold sex cells. When the male and female cells are mature, the sacs rupture, releasing the gametes into the water. The gametes fuse, grow, and finally develop into a new *Ascophyllum.* Upon emptying, unlike the sacs of the *Fucus,* those of *Ascophyllum* slough from the seaweed and are added to the food chain through the detrital cycle.

EXPLORATIONS

Note: Pterophycus, a west coast seaweed, can be substituted for *Ascophyllum* in the following growth investigations.

Growth Patterns in *Fucus*. *Fucus* growth is described as dichotomous, because one branch will divide into two branches. One division produces a Y; the next division produces a fork on each branch of the preceding growth.

Since this happens more or less annually, the general age of the weed can be determined by counting the number of branches. Since many of the weeds break easily, a perfectly symmetrical individual several years old is often difficult to find. Find several *Fucus* weeds. How many dichotomies can you count?

Where in the intertidal area do you find *Fucus* with the fewest branches? In the high-tide or low-tide area? Where do you find ones with the most branches? What can you infer about the habitat of *Fucus* and the life span of this seaweed? (See Chapter Note 6 for an explanation of its life span.)

Growth Rate in Brown Seaweeds. A brown seaweed that you can easily identify is *Ascophyllum nodosum*, or oarweed. It lacks an apparent midrib and it has obvious air bladders irregularly placed along its many slender branches. After a year or so, this seaweed annually forms one air bladder, or float, on each of its branches. By measuring the length between two bladders, you can determine how much the seaweed grew in one year. The most recent growth is that distance from the tip of the weed to the first bladder. In what year was the greatest growth and in what year was the least growth?

With the aid of your hand lens, examine the bladders. You may find holes in them, often due to the grazing action of snails. On occasion, researchers have recorded finding small marine animals taking up residence inside the floats. Can you find any squatters such as these?

On the west coast, look for the big brown kelp called *Pterophycus*. This algae displays growth rings. The space between the rings indicates the amount the seaweed has grown in a year. In what year did the seaweed grow the most? In what year was the least growth?

Seaweed and Surf Conditions. While examining *Ascophyllum*, record the location of the seaweed and the surf conditions. Make a list of other macroalgae (seaweeds) that may be growing in the same area. Look under the blanket of *Ascophyllum* that covers the rocks for the animals that live there. What animals did you find?

Seaweed and the Strand Line. You've probably noticed dried seaweed that has been tossed up on the beach and is among the debris stranded there by a high tide. Can seaweeds survive this? Do different kinds of algae dry at the same or different rates? To find out, you will need a fistful of each of three or four different kinds of seaweeds. You will also need a scale similar to those used in elementary school science classrooms, or a kitchen scale such as those used to measure food portions, and a piece of aluminum foil to hold your seaweeds on the balance pan. If you have to carry the seaweeds some distance from the beach, wrap them in moist paper toweling and store them in a cooler.

When you are ready to work with them, remove the seaweeds from their wrappings. Shake and blot excess water from each specimen. Make a little tray out of aluminum foil for the algae. Weigh the tray and record its weight. Place one specimen in the tray on the balance pan and weigh it. To determine the weight of the seaweed, subtract the weight of the empty aluminum tray from the weight of the tray plus the seaweed. Record the weight along with the time and date of the weighing.

Proceed in a similar manner for each of your specimens. Then put all of the weighed specimens on a tray and let them dry in direct sunlight. At breakfast, lunch, and dinnertime, weigh the seaweeds and record the weights. Do this until there is no change in weight. For some species, this may take several days. What is the survival advantage to seaweed of this slow drying? You can make a graph that shows the rate of drying for each species of algae.

Try to do this exploration with several different species of seaweeds. Be sure each specimen of seaweed weighs about the same to start with. How do the different species compare in drying time?

Seaweeds in the strand line will remain out of the water for as long as two

RATE OF DRYING FOR A PARTICULAR SPECIES OF SEAWEED

Name of Seaweed: _____

(Use *Ascophyllum* or any other species of seaweed available to you.)

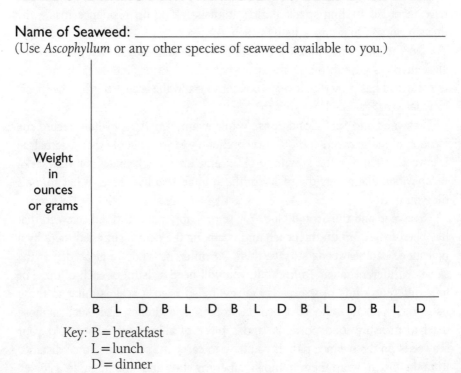

Weight in ounces or grams

B L D B L D B L D B L D B L D

Key: B = breakfast
L = lunch
D = dinner

weeks between spring tides. Do different species of seaweeds absorb water at the same rate? Put seaweeds of equal weight into separate jars containing equal amounts of seawater. Remove each from the water and weigh it at equal intervals. How long is it before the seaweeds stop absorbing water (gaining weight)?

CHAPTER NOTES

I. **Varieties of Red Seaweeds.** *Gigartina*, often confused with its relative *Chondrus crispus* (Irish moss), can generally be identified by a nubby texture, which is lacking in *Chondrus crispus*. You will often find *Gigartina* in the strand line on both northeast and northwest coasts, but *Chondrus* is a New England coastal dweller. Like *Chondrus*, *Gigartina* is often sunbleached, but *Gigartina* in this condition is quite unhealthy.

Another red seaweed found in the low-tide regions of both coasts is *Corallina*. The feathery branches of this delicate seaweed are covered with a crusty coat of calcium and magnesium carbonate. This seaweed is also found in the strand line, where it is bleached by the sun.

2. **A Brief Comparison between Seaweeds and Land Plants.**

A. *Holdfast:* Since they grow in water, seaweeds do not need the specialized roots, stem, and leaves of land plants. Land plants use their roots to anchor them in the soil and to absorb water and nutrients from the soil. Since seaweeds are immersed in their nutrient supply, their holdfast serves primarily to keep them in one spot, so that they do not get washed ashore or into deep water.

B. *Stipe:* The stems of land plants contain structures necessary to carry the raw materials from the roots to the leaves where photosynthesis takes place, and to carry the manufactured food to all living parts of the plant. The stipe, unique to a group of brown seaweeds called kelp, does not transport nutrients or raw materials; therefore, seaweeds don't need the complicated transport structures of the tree trunk or land plant stem. The tree trunk or plant stem also serves to support the leaves, holding them up in the sunlight. The stipe serves a similar function, supporting the blades and joining them to the holdfast; however, the stipe is not stiff like a stem or trunk.

C. *Blades:* The blades of seaweeds are somewhat analogous to leaves on trees and other land plants. Leaves of land plants are made of a complicated network of conducting tissues, which seaweeds lack, since they can remove the necessary raw material from the surrounding seawater.

3. Interactions. The interactions between living things also contribute to the formation of the zones that are characteristic of the intertidal region. The grazing by periwinkles on intertidal algae and the removal of barnacles by limpets from the intertidal zone are but two of these interactions. What other interactions do you observe that might shape the pattern of zonation in your area?

4. Diagram of Zones (Rocky Shore).

5. A Brief Look at Some Photosynthetic Adaptations. *Fucus spiralis* lacks air bladders. Since it lives high in the mid-tidal region, it is exposed to the sunlight for longer periods of time than those seaweeds living further down in the intertidal zone. Thus, it does not need to be buoyed up to receive enough sunlight for photosynthesis to take place.

Fucus vesiculosus and *Ascophyllum nodosum* live in the lower regions of the intertidal zone. Consequently, without a system of floats to hold them at the water's surface or just below it, these weeds would be exposed to sunlight for a shorter period of time than those seaweeds living higher in the intertidal region. Floats solve the problem of the plants' receiving enough sunlight by simply holding the seaweeds at or very close to the surface where light energy is sufficient for the food-making process.

6. Effects of Wave Action on Growth and Life Span. Variations in *Fucus* size are generally determined by the degree of exposure to wave action. *Fucus* that lives on exposed rocky shores will be smaller and shorter than one growing in a sheltered area. On these high-energy coastlines, *Fucus* growth is sparse.

CHAPTER 6

The Periwinkle

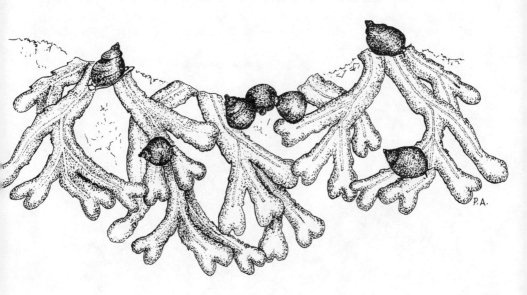

HUMBLE GRAZER

Periwinkles have been described as unattractive, dirty, dingy, dark, grimy, and even fuliginous. But periwinkles are a large group of small snails that have been inconspicuous, yet successful, residents of the rocky shore community for millions of years. Their genus name, *Littorina*, refers to the zone that lies between the high- and low-water marks at the seashore, where many of these gastropods make their home.

Because of their unappealing appearance, it's often a surprise to discover that for hundreds of years, *Littorina littorea*, or the common periwinkle, has been broiled and boiled, roasted and toasted, served from city pushcarts to the elegant tables of the best European restaurants. Archaeologists have uncovered periwinkle shells in ancient middens, or trash piles, in the British Isles and in other northern European coastal communities, indicating that these snails had been used as food even in primitive cultures.

At low tide along the rocky shore, hordes of periwinkles can be seen grazing upon the thin film of diatoms and other tiny algae that carpet the rock surface and veil the fronds of *Ulva*, *Fucus*, and other intertidal seaweeds. The radula, or file-like tongue, a structure common to snails (gastropods), is especially suited to the job of removing algae. The radula is a ribbon of hard protein located in the muscular pharynx that lies just behind the snail's mouth. Often described as a "coiled watch spring," the radula is controlled by the interactions of a complex array of muscles. Although the periwinkle grows to only one and one-half inches in height, its radula reaches an astonishing four to five inches in length. It is studded with microscopic teeth, and a very patient scientist counted about thirty-five hundred of them in a common periwinkle

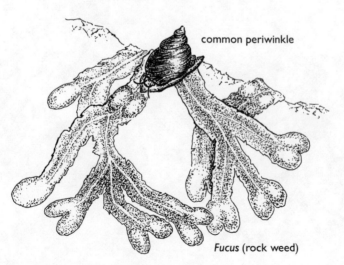

common periwinkle

Fucus (rock weed)

Common periwinkle grazing on Fucus

(*L. littorea*). As the teeth are worn smooth from use, they are replaced by a new set of teeth, which the snail rolls forward as needed.

Periwinkles generally feed when covered with water and as the tide is ebbing. During the last few hours of the falling tide, and with increased exposure to wind and sun, however, periwinkles become less active. Some of them retreat to the protection of the cool, damp seams and crevices of rocks, where they may continue grazing. Those that are left exposed on the coastal rock fields call into use another protective mechanism that is available to all marine snails. Each of them has an operculum, or disc-shaped trapdoor, that seals it tightly into its shell. Secreted by special glands located in the snail's large muscular foot, the operculum has several lifesaving functions. The disc is made of a tough protein similar to the material in our own fingernails. When the snail coils itself into its shell, the operculum seals off the opening. Seawater remains trapped inside with sufficient oxygen dissolved in it to keep the snail alive until the return of tidal waters with a new supply of life-sustaining oxygen. The water trapped within the shell also serves to lubricate the snail body. You will not find an operculum on the garden snail. Garden snails live in moist areas away from direct sunlight. This is a particularly handy mechanism for survival when suitable hiding places are not available. The land-based cousin of the periwinkle, the common garden snail, has no need for an operculum. Therefore, through evolution, the gland that produces the trapdoor has been eliminated.

Eons ago, in the warm Ordovician waters, all snails were tied to the sea. This nurturing, liquid mother provided them with food, shelter, and a medium for reproduction. Instead of coming together to mate, the snails release egg and sperm into the water. Tidal currents bring the two cells together. Then the resulting offspring are swept by the ocean currents to distant environments where new colonies are established.

Over time, however, the grip of the sea can grow weak. Scientists tell us that periwinkles illustrate the stages in evolutionary development from water-dependent creatures to land dwellers. Among the different clans of periwinkles that inhabit the Atlantic coastline, the three species that are representative of this process of leaving the sea for the land are the smooth periwinkle (*L. obtusata*), a total water dweller; the common periwinkle (*L. littorea*), which spends a few hours of each tidal cycle exposed to air; and the rough periwinkle (*L. saxitalis*), which can spend almost all of its time ashore.

If you can spend a few hours at the rocky shore, arrive at low tide and patiently root among the fronds of seaweeds, such as *Fucus* and *Ascophyllum*. You are likely to find the tiniest members of the periwinkle tribe. With their

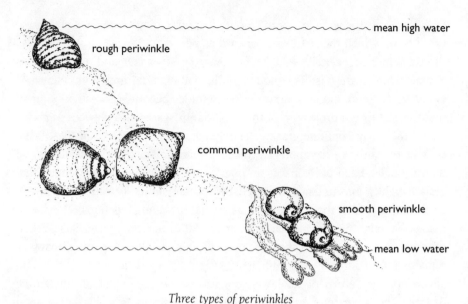

mean high water

rough periwinkle

common periwinkle

smooth periwinkle

mean low water

Three types of periwinkles

delicate, round shells in various shades of green, yellow, orange, and brown, the smooth periwinkles *(L. obtusata)* are well concealed among the weeds that nourish and protect them.

Still completely tied to the sea, these winkles are exposed to the air by only the lowest of the low tides, which occur twice monthly. Even during these times of brief exposure, the snails remain nestled among the damp, protective curtains of seaweed fronds, since their delicate gill structure, designed for extracting oxygen from seawater, cannot function when exposed to air.

You may make another interesting discovery in this low-tide area. These minute periwinkles lay eggs. Fertilized as they are spawned, the eggs are wrapped in globs of protective jelly. As further protection, the egg packets are fastened to the surrounding weeds, where the young find shelter when they emerge and where you may find the jelly masses.

The next area to explore is a bit up from the low-tide zone. This is the intertidal space where the largest and the most abundant periwinkle, the common periwinkle *(L. littorea)*, lives. This large brown herbivore dominates the area that extends halfway up the intertidal zone of the rocky shore, an area that is briefly submerged twice daily by tidal waters. The respiratory structures of this species are so designed that the common periwinkle can spend more time out of the water than underwater. However, since the common periwinkle's eggs and sperm are shed directly into the sea and fertilization of these gametes depends on tidal currents, their link to the sea is still strong.

THE ROCKY SHORE

The shells of the common periwinkles are large (from one to one and one-half inches high), somewhat pointed, and gray to gray-brown. They present a sharp contrast to the one-half-inch, rounded, smooth shells of the smooth periwinkles. Since the common periwinkle has been known to sharply reduce populations of algae, they are presently being studied for the impact their grazing has on marsh development. Some scientists think that they may slow or prevent the development of marsh areas.

Further landward in the intertidal zone, you will find the rough periwinkles (*L. saxitalis*). These have established their kingdom in the region of the intertidal zone that is reached only by the highest of the high tides. A soaking every two weeks is sufficient contact with the sea for them to function efficiently. Instead of a gill system that extracts oxygen from seawater, a gill chamber has developed that functions, at least partially, as a lung, capable of removing oxygen from the air. An occasional drenching by spring tides is sufficient to keep the chamber moist, but long submersion will drown these snails. You will recognize these snails, as they graze on rocks covered with blue-green algae, by their dark gray or brown shells with spiral ridges.

The rough periwinkle has eliminated its reproductive need for water. Fertilization takes place internally, and the young develop in a brood pouch kept within the mother. When fully developed, the young snails emerge replete with spiral shells. You may find them hiding in deserted barnacle shells or in the empty shells of clams and mussels.

THE WORLD OF THE PERIWINKLE

What you will need
basic kit
large, wide-mouthed jar
bucket
glass pie plate or stiff piece
  of transparent plastic

Science skills
observing
comparing
inferring

OBSERVATIONS

How to Find the Periwinkle. Periwinkles have been studied extensively by scientists investigating the special animal adaptations that are necessary for survival in the intertidal zone. You can begin your study of these interesting animals by observing the common periwinkle, *Littorina littorea*, one of the three types found along the rocky shore. The range of the common periwinkle in the intertidal zone is extensive. Since periwinkles wander over most of the

PERIWINKLE COUSINS

Zone	Atlantic Coast	Pacific Coast
Spray	*Littorina saxitalis* (rough periwinkle) Range: Labrador to Maryland	*Littorina keena* (erroded periwinkle) Range: Puget Sound to Baja California
Mid-Tide	*Littorina littorea* (common periwinkle) Range: Labrador to Maryland	*Littorina scutula* (checkered periwinkle) Range: Alaska to Baja California
Low-Tide	*Littorina obtusata* (smooth periwinkle) Range: Labrador to New Jersey	*Littorina sitkana* (sitka periwinkle) Range: Northern Alaska to Southern Oregon

Species of periwinkles occupying similar niches on different coastlines.

area between mean high water and mean low water, this rather large marine snail is the easiest of the three types to locate. As you explore among the rocks at low tide, you may notice that some snails, like the mud snail, have pointed shells but that those on the rocks are more rounded. The dark color of the common periwinkle blends well with the rocks. The larger common periwinkles can be about one and one-half inches in height and they are somewhat pointed.

Gently remove a periwinkle from the surface of a rock. Look closely at the opening of the snail's shell. With your fingernail or a small piece of dry grass, very gently touch the disc that covers the opening. How does the snail respond? How does this disc feel? (See Chapter Note 1 for a brief discussion of the operculum.)

Snail Tentacles. Put the snail onto a firm, flat surface. A glass pie plate or a stiff piece of clear, transparent plastic will do nicely. As the snail adjusts to this new environment, it will come out of its shell slowly and begin to explore its surroundings. Examine the snail's head. Use your hand lens and look closely at the miniature "horns." These are sensory devices. Watch the snail for a while and observe how it uses its tentacles.

The Radula. Periwinkles are the dominant herbivores, or grass eaters, of the intertidal zone. To see their efficient, rasping tongue, or radula, hold the plastic sheet so that you can see the snail's foot. With a little patience, you will probably observe the radula scraping the plastic sheet.

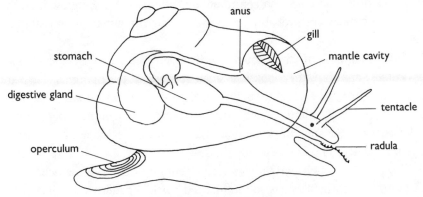

A look inside the periwinkle

EXPLORATIONS

A Snail Aquarium. If you would like to observe the snail and its behavior in more detail, you can keep a few snails in a small "aquarium." Select a wide-mouthed jar or bucket. Fill the jar half full of seawater, and add some small stones and some seaweed from the intertidal zone. Leave the jar in a sunny spot for a few days, so that a film of algae can develop on the sides of the jar. To replace the water lost through evaporation, you may have to add some fresh seawater to your jar. You may find that the mini-aquarium will not survive without some aeration, which you can provide with a small aquarium air pump. After a few days, you probably will have many opportunities to see the snail's radula, or rasping tongue, as it scrapes the algae from the sides of the jar.

Tidal Memory of the Common Periwinkle. When you observe the mini-aquarium, note how many snails are grazing on the glass above the level of the water. Can you make any inferences about how much of their time they spend out of the water? Do you think this behavior might be related to the amount of time they spend out of the water between low and high tide?

The Effects of Grazing on Seaweed Growth. You may observe the periwinkles in your mini-aquarium grazing on the surface of the seaweed. They are feeding on microalgae growing on the seaweed. Periwinkles can scrape rocks clean of their algal growth. Their eating activity has also been known to significantly reduce populations of larger seaweeds, such as leafy *Ulva* (sea lettuce) and the tubular strands of *Enteromorpha* (gut weed). Visit a section of the intertidal zone where there aren't any periwinkles. Do you find a substantial amount of algae and larger seaweeds growing on the rocks? Visit another area where periwinkles are abundant. Assuming that other herbivores are absent or that their numbers are too small to make an impact on the growth of algae, what do you observe to be the effect of periwinkles on algal growth?

While other variables also contribute to a decrease in algal growth on the rocks, periwinkles are probably the primary "lawn mowers" of the intertidal zone.

Tidal Memory of the Rough Periwinkle. When rough periwinkles (*L. saxitalis*) are born, they look like small versions of their parents. They are equipped at birth to graze the pastures of algae-coated rocks that line the high zones of the rocky shore. Unlike their cousins, the common periwinkles (*L. littorea*) and the smooth periwinkles (*L. obtusata*), they do not have a larval stage that needs to be nourished by the sea.

However, the rough periwinkles are not entirely free from the hold of the sea. Some of their behavior is still influenced by tidal patterns. Scientists have discovered that rough periwinkles "remember" the tidal cycle for months after their removal from the intertidal zone. You can see this "memory" at work by observing some rough periwinkles in your mini-aquarium for a two-week period.

Rough periwinkles are most active during the spring tides that occur during the full moon and new moon phases of the lunar cycle. During the remaining phases of the lunar cycle, rough periwinkles are quite lethargic. You can find out when the spring tides will occur by checking the weather pages of your local newspaper.

A few days before the next spring tide, collect some rough periwinkles and put them into your mini-aquarium. Observe the snails several times each day before the spring tides, keeping notes. Describe their behavior at the time of the very high tides. Are they more or less active? Describe their location in the mini-aquarium. Does their location seem to be related to the state of the tide?

CHAPTER NOTES

I. The Operculum, or Trapdoor. The operculum is also a shield for the periwinkle that provides the soft-bodied snail with protection from predators. However, neither shell nor operculum can entirely protect the snail from all of its predators all of the time. Some predators, such as sandpipers and plovers, can penetrate the operculum. Man, another dangerous predator, can also open the tasty periwinkle.

PART II

THE
SALT MARSH
AND THE
MUD FLATS

I N ONE OF the great classics of American literature, *Evangeline*, Henry Wadsworth Longfellow introduces us to the Acadians, who were among the first Europeans to settle in North America. These French colonists built their homes, churches, roads, and farms beside the great salt meadows of the Bay of Fundy. They established a network of villages, the largest of which was at Grand Pré, Nova Scotia. Longfellow's narrative poem recounts the tragic events that led to the destruction of the settlements and that uprooted this gentle people who had lived in harmony with the land and with the Indians for more than 150 years.

The secret of the Acadian prosperity was simple. They recognized the natural productivity of the salt marshes and exploited that productivity without harming the integrity of the marshes. Their insight and respect for the marshes were repaid with a cornucopia of hay for their livestock, as well as muskrat, fish, waterfowl, and shellfish for their tables. Furthermore, they harvested fields of flax and corn, and they lived in peace and contentment.

It may come as a surprise to many people to find that tidal marshes flourish in the far north, even along the bays and coves of the Arctic. These ribbons of life even wind along the coasts of Ellesmere Island north of the Arctic Circle. They grow out from the protected shores of Hudson Bay and on the coastline of Baffin Island. For a few short weeks, these green fringes provide shelter and food for thousands of nesting birds, such as willets, knots, turnstones, and the very large group of birds called sandpipers. These are the birds that visit our coastal marshes during their fall and spring migrations.

You will also find salt marshes flourishing along the coast of Nova Scotia, the Bay of Fundy, and the shoreline of New Brunswick. Isolated patches of marshlands are to be found on the otherwise rocky coast of Maine, but broader expanses of wetlands cover the shallow bays of Massachusetts, Rhode Island, Connecticut, and New York. Scientists refer to these marshes as the "Arctic," the "Bay of Fundy," and the "New England," respectively.

Spawned from a different glacial and geological history, these northern marshes cannot rival the spectacular tidelands to the south that form an almost continuous grassy belt from New Jersey to northern Florida. These wetlands, known as the Atlantic coastal plain and Gulf of Mexico marshes, have developed behind long chains of barrier islands, which protect them from the full onslaught of an angry sea. Thus protected, the salt marshes are also less vulnerable to gentle, but constant, tidal erosion. The marshes of Louisiana and

Tropic of Cancer

■ salt marsh

Location of salt marshes in North America

Georgia, often considered the most spectacular display of wetlands, stand apart from all others in acreage and awesome beauty. It is these marshes that have been immortalized in the well-known poem, "The Marshes of Glynn," written by Sidney Lanier in 1877. Delaware Bay and the eastern shore of the Chesapeake Bay also support huge, productive marshlands.

The west coast north of San Francisco is host to relatively few salt marshes. The largest in this area are found along the Arctic shores of Alaska. South of

San Francisco, where the shoreline is less rocky, salt marshes are found in the bays and estuaries, especially in the Baja California region.

Regardless of the location of tidal wetlands, the mechanisms that form them are essentially similar. Carrying sand and silt from neighboring shores, as well as material churned up from the ocean floor, the twice-daily incoming tides bring sediment-rich seawater into the shallows. As the water flows into coves and inlets, its forward motion slows considerably. When this happens, the freight of sand and mud carried in suspension by the water is released. Much of the load settles to the bottom close to shore. As long as these deposits continue and sea level doesn't rise, mud flats form and are exposed at low tide.

When the height of the mud reaches mid-tide level, seeds of *Spartina alterniflora* and other salt-tolerant plants carried by birds, wind, and tidal currents establish a foothold. Once solidly rooted, the plants have the effect of further slowing the flow of water over the surface of the mud. Isolated hummocks of plants soon dot the mud flats. These small, grassy knolls slowly spread out and finally cover the entire mud flat. As mud flats continue to develop in the shallow water seaward of the marsh, the grasses slowly move forward and extend the newer marsh. Meanwhile, established marsh plants grow, die, and decay, and in the process, build up the level of the older marsh.

The shoreward side of the marsh eventually gives way to other land plants, such as seaside goldenrod, salt marsh aster, and marsh orach. In time, groundsel trees, marsh elder, and other bushes take hold of their share of the marsh; and finally, bear oaks, pitch pines, and other trees lay claim to the upland portion of the marsh.

River deposits also contribute to developing marshlands. Flowing water, coursing through riverbeds, erodes rock material and carries it seaward along with suspended soil particles. Upon reaching the spreading river mouths, the speed at which the water has been flowing decreases, and the sediment suspended in the water column is deposited, forming mud flats. Rivers contributing to the marshes in the Northeast and in the Mid-Atlantic region course through erosion-resistant granite and basalt. The major rivers of this area are the St. Lawrence River, flowing from the Great Lakes; the St. John River, with its source in northern Maine; the Connecticut River, flowing through New England into Long Island Sound; and the Hudson River, draining the Hudson and Mohawk valleys. The Delaware River and the Susquehanna River contribute water and sediment to the Delaware Bay and the Chesapeake Bay, respectively. These northern rivers carry considerably less sediment than those flowing through Appalachian Mountain river valleys, which are lined with softer sedimentary rocks.

Some of the rivers running through softer sedimentary rock that contribute to marsh development in the South include the Santee River of South Carolina, the Savannah River in Georgia, and the Pee Dee, which begins its seaward journey in the mountains of North Carolina.

Although there are many rivers that contribute sediment to developing coastal marshes, when it comes to carrying water and alluvium, the muddy Mississippi River is the diva of American waterways. Tide marshes and mud flats that have formed in the delta of this mighty watercourse are of breathtaking beauty, and like all other healthy tide marshes, support enormous numbers of wildlife species.

The third category of tidal wetlands includes those marshes that occur along the Pacific coast. The extensive salt marshes of the Alaskan coast and those of Baja, California belong to this group. Other major marshes of the Pacific coast are in protected embayments such as San Francisco Bay and the hundreds of coves that weave along the wrinkled, rocky coasts of Oregon and Washington.

As coastal communities continued to develop during the early history of New World immigration, those colonists who settled along the mid-Atlantic coast and to the south were not as careful with the land as the early settlers of Acadia. This newer wave of people vigorously farmed the land, drained the marshes, depleted the soil, and watched the weakened earth erode into crystal clear streams and rivers. Our more recent history shows an even more shortsighted attitude toward our precious wetlands. We have "developed" (or destroyed) over 70 percent of the salt marshes of the Northeast, and we have defiled those that remain with twentieth century debris.

In the pages that follow, you'll have an opportunity to discover some of the fascinating creatures that make their homes in tidal wetlands. By participating in the suggested activities, you can learn some of the secrets that make tidal wetlands such valuable natural resources. Perhaps you will also come to treasure the peaceful beauty of the marshes.

CHAPTER 7

The Fiddler Crab

CAVE DWELLER OF THE MARSH

As the tide ebbs along the banks of marsh creeks and drainage canals, hordes of nimble, spider-like creatures emerge from holes that riddle the peat banks. They scuttle along the mud flats and among the stiff green spears of marsh grass (*Spartina alterniflora*), feasting on the banquet of organic matter so generously served by the sea. These swift, agile creatures are crustaceans called fiddler crabs (*Uca pugnax*). The sun-loving fiddlers are dark brown, making them inconspicuous against the mud they inhabit. Their presence is often first detected by the crackling sounds they make as they scurry to and fro claiming their share of the bounty.

The most distinguishing physical feature of the fiddler is the oversized claw of the male, which constitutes 40 percent of his body weight. This claw is useless for feeding and, in fact, puts the male at a distinct disadvantage when the food arrives, since he can only grab his meals with the smaller claw. However, what he lacks in utensils, he makes up for in speed and aggression, as he shovels in gobs of mud twice as fast as his female dinner companion. Since the male's energy requirements are not as high as the egg-laying female's, having only one feeding claw is not a nutritional disadvantage.

Fiddler crabs are deposit feeders; they feed on decaying pieces of cord-grass and other organic material, such as algae, fungi, and bacteria, which settles on the marsh mud as the tide recedes. Fiddlers have a complex mouth that is surrounded by six pairs of modified, bristle-covered "legs." The feeding claws pass spoonfuls of mud to these legs, which scrape nutrient material from the heavier granular particles. The edible matter then floats and is easier to swallow. The coarser material that remains is later rolled into little balls, neatly spit into a claw, and returned to the marsh surface.

Fiddlers must have an external source of water in order to eat. Therefore, as the marsh surface begins to dry, mealtime comes to an end well before the return of the tide. A great deal of shoving and trampling occurs in the crab neighborhood as fiddlers beat a hasty retreat to their burrows so that, with the help of trapdoors, they can make themselves snug inside before the incoming tide.

The burrow, the center of the fiddler's life, is dug in the peat along the banks of a marsh creek. Each burrow is a tunnel two to three feet long, dug diagonally downward and barely wide enough to let the occupant pass.

The crab excavates his home by digging and scraping sand and mud with his walking legs, the four pairs of legs behind the pinching claws. The loose soil is then rolled into balls, pushed out through the entrance of the burrow, and carried to the surface of the marsh. A newly developed crab "condo" can be identified by little piles of black balls heaped some distance from the burrow openings. Male crabs, usually dissatisfied with their new homes, generally move throughout the community looking for a place to live that is more to their liking. They seek out the burrows of smaller and more timid crabs. Then the aggressor, standing by the entrance to the tunnel, brandishes his super-sized claw in a threatening manner. The homeowner, intimidated by this behavior, makes a quick getaway. The displaced crab, not to be left without a place to live, repeats this scene at the burrow of a less fortunate neighbor. Thus, throughout the crab community, there is a constant shifting of crabs from burrow to burrow, accompanied by constant digging and remodeling. Evidence of tunneling and redistribution of soil is almost always apparent on the marsh surface. The whole scene is not unlike the mobility of suburban life.

Fiddlers spend the winter snug in their burrows in a state resembling hibernation, while the season takes its toll on their homes. Freezing and thawing of the ground causes soil and detritus from dead and decaying plant roots to accumulate in the crab burrows. By the time spring arrives, debris blocks the tunnels. During April or May, when the temperature in the burrows reaches sixty degrees or so, the crabs emerge, en masse, above the ground.

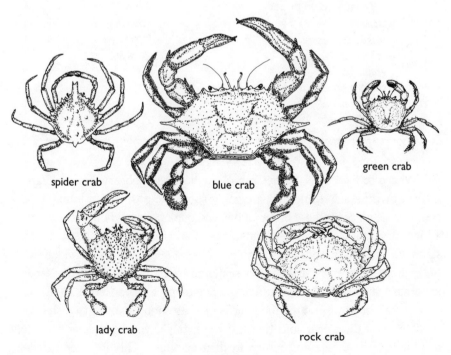

spider crab

blue crab

green crab

lady crab

rock crab

Relatives of the fiddler crab

With winter over, they begin the arduous job of repairing damaged burrows. They scrape and they dig; they carry the spoils of their excavations to the marsh surface where they deposit them.

Research shows that fiddler crabs and salt marsh cordgrass enjoy a mutually beneficial relationship. The intense burrowing activity of the crabs increases above-ground production of marsh grass by helping the plants to grow more vigorously and to produce more seeds. Additionally, the underground activity of the fiddlers mixes marsh mud, aerates it, and drains the soil. Finally, their tunneling aids in decomposing dead plant material that has accumulated below the ground. In return for their efforts, the crabs are supplied with structural support for their burrows. The root system of the cordgrass provides a thatched roof.

Of course, the story of the fiddler crabs and the marsh doesn't end here. Fiddlers are food for many marsh birds, such as herons and egrets. They are also a favorite delicacy on the menu of the blue crabs, which are in turn enjoyed by many of us.

THE WORLD OF THE FIDDLER CRAB

What you will need
basic kit
plastic containers
scoop net
graph paper
camera with telephoto lens
(optional)
nimble fingers

Science skills
observing
inferring
graphing

OBSERVATIONS

Where to Find the Fiddler Crab. A good place to observe fiddler crabs is in their own habitat while they are going about the business of living. Find a comfortable place for these observations and explorations where you can sit on a high, dry spot close to a salt marsh mud flat. Search at low tide. Look for a stand of salt marsh cordgrass (*Spartina alterniflora*), and you'll undoubtedly find hundreds of tiny crab burrows scattered in the marsh peat. Another way to locate the burrows is to paddle a canoe along a marsh creek. You'll find fiddler crab burrows dotting the peat banks. As soon as you arrive, the crabs probably will disappear into their burrows, but if you wait quietly without moving, they'll surface and return to their activities. This is a good time to observe feeding, fighting, and other behaviors. A camera with a telephoto lens will be helpful in recording the variety of behaviors. If you don't have this piece of equipment, a notebook and pencil will do nicely. (See Chapter Note 1 for information on the California fiddler.)

Crab Burrows. Select a few crab burrow openings and examine them. Does there seem to be any order to their arrangement or are they scattered randomly on the marsh mud and on the banks of marsh creeks? How close together are the burrows? Do they vary in size? Look for the tiny balls of mud that often lie beside the burrow opening. How many of the burrows seem to be in use? What clues did you use?

Evidence of Feeding. Fiddler crabs feed on the nutrient material deposited on the surface of salt marsh mud. Examine the surface of the mud around the opening of the crab burrows. Look for scrape marks made by foraging crabs as their small claws pick up food left by the tide.

Who Eats Whom. Although fiddler crabs are enjoyable to watch, their role in a variety of food chains makes them important subjects of scientific study. As you watch them moving out of their burrows and scurrying about, you will eventually see some of them feeding. If you are lucky, you may see one of their predators attempt to dine upon a fiddler crab. Note the reaction of fiddlers to danger. Does the reaction seem to be an individual reaction or a group reaction? You may notice that when one fiddler emerges from a burrow, many others quickly emerge. Does the presence of large numbers of fiddlers on the mud make it easier for predators or more difficult? (See Chapter Note 2 for a partial list of predators that dine at the "fiddler raw bar.")

Based on your observations, what is the role of fiddler crabs in the food chains of the salt marsh? (See Chapter Note 3 for some specific links in marsh food chains.)

Observing Social Interactions. As you observe the fiddler crabs, pay special attention to how they interact with each other. How close do they come to each other? Do they face each other? What behaviors accompany this meeting? Do you see any evidence of what might be called hostile behavior? Carefully documented observations of social animals are an important aspect of current scientific research.

Mating behavior among the fiddler crabs occurs when spring comes to the marsh. After you have gained some experience observing, try to watch a crab population at mating time. Does there seem to be a pattern in the way the males wave their large claws? Describe this pattern in your notes. How does the male seem to use his oversized claw in interactions with other males? Is it used differently in interactions with females? Does it seem to be used as a weapon to defend his territory or as a challenge to other males? Do females seem to exhibit any response behaviors that are different from male response behaviors?

Other Members of the Salt Marsh Community. Make a list of other animals that live in the salt marsh community. As you investigate the world of fiddler crabs, you will become aware of some food chains. Record these chains and try to see links between various chains. The links enable you to construct a food web.

EXPLORATIONS

What Fiddler Crabs See. Fiddler eyes are on retractable stalks and are controlled by a complicated set of muscles. Although fiddler crabs cannot distinguish shapes, they are extremely sensitive to movement. How sensitive are these eyes? Sit very still until the crabs are unaware of your presence. With a piece of dead grass in hand, slowly move it toward a crab from behind, from the side, and from in front of the crab. How close can you get before the crab scuttles away? Do crab eyes seem to "see" equally well from all directions? How much movement do you have to make to set off the danger alarm in the group?

The Reaction of Fiddlers to Vibrations. Do crabs detect vibrations as well as movement? Begin tapping the ground several feet away from the crab. Continue tapping the ground as you move closer to the crab, but be careful to keep all motion to a minimum. How close can you get before the crab scurries away? What are the hunting behaviors of their predators? Which sense do you think the crab uses to detect its predators?

Different Types of Fiddler Crabs. There are three eastern species of fiddler crabs, each with its own habitat preference. *Uca minx* prefers the brackish water found near the flow of fresh water entering the marsh estuary. *Uca pugnax*, the mud fiddler, is found in salt marshes, and *Uca pugilator* can be seen in sandier areas of the seashore. Look in these different habitats and see if you can find a fiddler of each type, trap it, and put each in its own container. Compare them with each other. How are they alike and how are they different? Consult your field guide for accurate identification.

Are Crabs Right-Handed or Left-Handed? Most male fiddler crabs are right-handed: the right claw is the larger of the two claws. It is unusual to find many males whose left claws are oversized, but in some colonies almost half of the males are left-handed. How many left-handed fiddlers do you observe? How many are right-handed? How many crabs have only one claw? What is the relationship between body size and claw length? Since fiddlers are often difficult to catch, you may have to estimate. What is the frequency of right-handed fiddlers, left-handed fiddlers, and one-claw fiddlers in your popula-

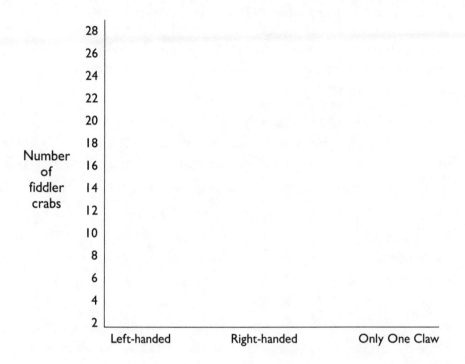

FREQUENCY OF HANDEDNESS IN A POPULATION OF FIDDLER CRABS (MALES)

Number of fiddler crabs

| 28 |
| 26 |
| 24 |
| 22 |
| 20 |
| 18 |
| 16 |
| 14 |
| 12 |
| 10 |
| 8 |
| 6 |
| 4 |
| 2 |

Left-handed   Right-handed   Only One Claw

tion? To indicate the frequency of each trait, make a histogram similar to the one above. If your population is not very large, you could find the percentage of right-handed, left-handed, and one-claw fiddlers in the group.

CHAPTER NOTES

1. **The California Fiddler.** The California fiddler, *Uca crenulata*, is the only fiddler crab on the west coast, and it is confined to the area from southern California to the Baja Peninsula. This species prefers to build its burrows in sandy mud close to the high-tide line. Like its eastern cousins, the male California fiddler has one oversized claw. Scientists tell us that the future of this little crab is uncertain due to large scale construction by humans in areas that are potential crab habitats. The observations and explorations suggested in this chapter can be carried out with the California fiddler.

2. **Predators of the Fiddler Crab.** Predators such as gulls, whimbrels, rails, ducks, and herons may make a meal out of some of the crabs you are watching. Raccoons and blue crabs are also excellent crabbers. Blue crabs can

always be expected to lie in ambush, cleverly concealed by *Spartina* stems, stones, and ribbed mussels.

3. Food Chains of the Salt Marsh. Fiddler crabs and other species of crabs are among the most important consumers in the detritus-based food chain. Detritus consists of the "leftovers," the bits and pieces of edibles and the partially digested food of other animal life. Fiddlers are able to convert plant material that most other consumers cannot digest into animal protein.

Three marsh food chains:

a. detritus > fiddler crabs > raccoons
b. detritus > fiddler crabs > herons
c. detritus > fiddler crabs > blue crabs > us

CHAPTER 8

The Horseshoe Crab

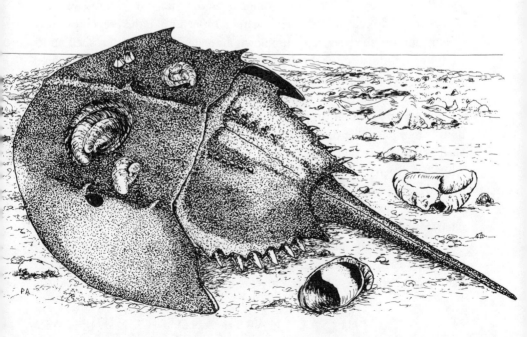

AN ANCIENT TRAVELER

It's spring and the sun slowly warms the waters of bays and estuaries along the Atlantic coast. Meanwhile, far offshore and buried in the dark, protective world within the sediment that covers the ocean floor, life begins to stir. Somehow, without the aid of seasonal cues, such as changes in temperature and the increase in daylight hours, strange, reclusive creatures are about to wake from their winter torpor. Weeks prior to the highest of the high tides of May and June, these animals begin to tug free from the tender hold of soft mud hundreds of feet beneath the ocean's surface. Thus, each year, horseshoe crabs begin an awesome spring ritual that originated in ancient seabeds about 500 million years ago. Since horseshoe crabs can winter as far as fifty miles offshore, the journey to their breeding grounds on protected beaches and mud flats is arduous; it can take as long as six to eight weeks.

These modern wanderers are identical to the horseshoe crabs that toured the shores in the age of the dinosaurs long ago, and their only close relatives are animals that have been extinct for millions of years. Fossil records tell us that horseshoe crabs, as they appear today, have survived significantly unchanged through the great extinctions and the geological catastrophes that have occurred since the age of the dinosaurs. This constancy in structure and behavior has earned these peaceful animals the grand accolade of being called "living fossils." Horseshoe crabs (Limulus polyphemus) belong to that extremely large and successful animal group called arthropods. Membership in this phylum makes them relatives of shrimps, insects, lobsters, and centipedes.

Prior to the early part of the twentieth century, horseshoe crabs were not always so neatly categorized. Even a careful observer like the French explorer Champlain saw the previously unknown animal as "a fish with a shell on its back like a tortoise. . . ." However, on the basis of some recently discovered specialized traits, scientists have assigned these enigmatic creatures to an order, Xiphosura, in which they are the only members, a lonely distinction.

Similar to other arthropods, horseshoe crabs have jointed legs. Additionally they have a hard, inelastic, brown carapace, or external skeleton, that is shed periodically to accommodate the growing animal. In the molting process, which is triggered by hormonal activity, all chitinous parts are shed, even the thin coverings over the eyes and gill books. When the crab emerges, it leaves behind the intact and unmistakable shed for the lucky beachcomber, who often thinks that he has found a dead horseshoe crab.

Horseshoe crabs may molt as many as five or six times during the first year. With each molt the crab grows about twenty to twenty-five percent. A mature carapace takes about seven years to develop; the crab probably sheds about twenty-five times in that period. During their "adolescent" molt, males develop specialized hook-shaped, grasping claws. With these pedipalps, the males can grab the lower portion of the female carapace in a sexual hug that may last throughout the mating season.

The body of the crab is divided into three regions. The wide cephalo-thorax, suggestive of a horseshoe, contains both the head and the visceral organs (the stomach, intestines, and liver). A flexible joint marks the beginning of the spine-bordered buckler that protects the crab's respiratory organs, or gill books. The pages of these books are thin tissues through which oxygen dissolved in seawater diffuses into the animal's blood system.

The gill books double as swimming appendages, and used in conjunction with its legs, they enable *Limulus* to perform an awkward but effective back-stroke. At the end of a swim, the crab settles to the sand at the bottom of the bay, but, unfortunately, it lands upside down, exposing its soft underparts to predators. However, the crab's long, tapered tail, which swivels on a ball-and-socket joint, can help save the crab's life. With a little struggle, *Limulus* thrusts its tail into the soft sand, wiggles somewhat, rights itself, and is again protected by its dome-shaped armor. Although the tail evokes fear in the uninformed, it does not secrete exotic toxins. It's not a weapon. Rather, it's a tool that is essential to the well-being of the animal, and its loss will result in the animal's death.

Horseshoe crabs have two sets of eyes. A pair of simple eyes can be found close together on the midline of the carapace. They are receptors that are sensitive to ultraviolet light from the moon. Working in harmony with a biological clock, the simple eyes trigger the annual shoreward migration of *Limulus*. Additionally, recent research shows that two kidney-shaped, com-pound eyes on top of the carapace respond to patterns of polarized light in the sky, indicating that *Limulus* uses a type of celestial navigation during the yearly trek toward shore.

In May when the offshore waters reach about fifty degrees, horseshoe crabs generally make their appearance in shallow bays. Initially, lone female crabs can be seen wandering across the sandy bottom. Soon males appear and outnumber the females by as many as five to one. Very shortly after their appearance, one or more of the males clip onto the first female that happens by. This grouping generally lasts throughout the four- to five-week egg-laying season.

Finally, with an incoming tide, a phalanx of armored "tanks" laboriously bulldozes its way up the beach to the place where the female will scrape a hollow in the sand. There she will lay her eggs and the male in tow will fertilize them. In making this trip, horseshoe crabs severely disturb the mud-flat community. They disrupt animal burrows and decimate populations of crustaceans, mollusks, worms, and other animals living just below the surface of the mud. This destruction occurs in part because of the way *Limulus* eats. Lacking true jaws, its mouthparts are attached to its legs. Stiff bristles, which cut food into tiny, manageable pieces before they enter the oral cavity, are attached to the five pairs of walking legs. These brushes extend from the elbow of each leg to its base. This design dictates that the animal eat only when moving.

On the retreating tide, battalions of horseshoe crabs will return to the sea, leaving behind their developing eggs in the moist, warm sand. As their ancestors have done throughout time, these crabs will then head back out to sea and again bury themselves in the sediment of the ocean floor to await the call of another spring. Although philosophers tell us that nothing endures but change, apparently *Limulus polyphemus* endures as well.

THE WORLD OF THE HORSESHOE CRAB

What you will need	Science skills
basic kit	*observing*
	recording
	comparing
	graphing
	measuring

OBSERVATIONS

The Horseshoe Crab Shed. The horseshoe crab molts by squeezing itself out of its external skeleton, leaving behind the complete exoskeleton, or shed. The exoskeleton splits open along the forward lower edge as the animal emerges. Find a shed on the beach and look for the slit along the leading curve. If you don't find the slit, you'll know you don't have a shed. Instead, you probably have the remains of a dead horseshoe crab. (See Chapter Note 1 for the range of *Limulus*.)

The Basic Anatomy of the Horseshoe Crab. You can use either a shed or a living horseshoe crab to identify the major parts of the animal. Use the accompanying diagram and find the median eyes, the lateral eyes, and the cephalothorax, which is the large portion of the shield. Locate the movable spines on the abdomen and the telson, or tail. Find a living crab to carry out the more detailed examination that follows.

A Close Look at All Those Legs. Using both hands, gently pick up a

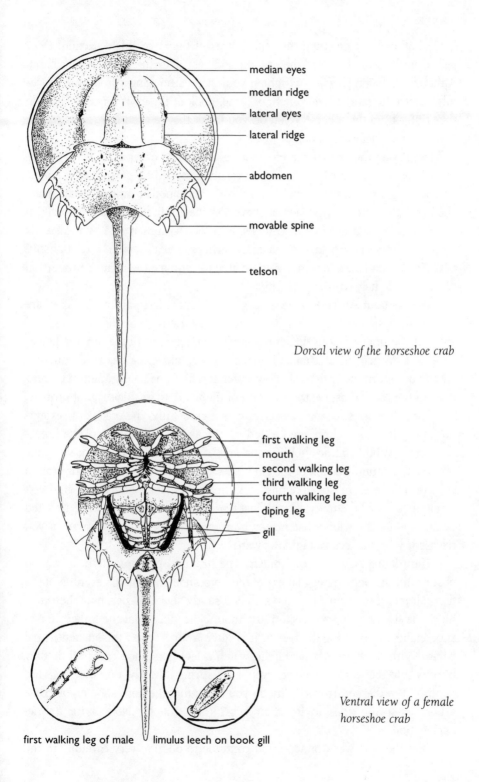

median eyes

median ridge

lateral eyes

lateral ridge

abdomen

movable spine

telson

Dorsal view of the horseshoe crab

first walking leg
mouth
second walking leg
third walking leg
fourth walking leg
diping leg

gill

first walking leg of male   limulus leech on book gill

*Ventral view of a female
horseshoe crab*

horseshoe crab by grasping the outer edges of the large shield section. *Don't pick it up by its tail!* Invert the animal and rest it in the palm of one hand. Although its flailing legs may frighten you, there is no danger from this peaceful creature; it cannot bite, pinch, or sting. Look at the front pincers. How do they differ from the others? What do you think they're used for? (See Chapter Note 2 for a brief explanation.)

Identifying the Sex of the Horseshoe Crab. The first pair of walking legs in male horseshoe crabs are hooks especially designed for grasping the female carapace. Is your animal a male or female? Find another animal or an intact shed and compare the first sets of claws. Do they indicate a male or female? If you can examine a number of animals, keep notes on their size by measuring each one from the tip to the tail end. Perhaps you can infer a relationship between sex and size. You may also be able to estimate the relative proportion of males to females in the population.

What About All Those Other Legs? Look at the last pair of legs. They are especially designed to prevent the crab from sinking into the sand as they shove the animal along in the jerking style characteristic of the moving horseshoe crab. Watch the animal as it makes its way along the beach. Frequently, when you return the crab to shallow water, it will immediately attempt to bury itself in the sand. Observe the function of the rear legs in this digging process.

The Gill Books. Using the diagram as a guide, find the organs of respiration, the gill books. These are located on the abdominal section of the horseshoe crab. While you are holding the crab in an inverted position, you may observe the flapping action of the gill books. This motion is used by the crab to achieve a little extra speed while swimming. You may notice the gill-book action if you hold the inverted crab just under the water's surface. The inverted position is used for long-distance swimming. Will the crab also swim if you release it with the legs facing downward?

The Mating Activities of *Limulus*. The first and perhaps the best time to observe the mating and egg laying of the horseshoe crabs is the evening of the first full moon in spring. If you watch at a sandy sheltered beach as the extra-high tide floods in over the sand, the moonlight will reveal the linked horseshoe crabs approaching the beach. It is quite a thrill to see this ancient ritual begin. With the help of a flashlight, watch a few horseshoe crabs while they burrow into the wet sand at the level of the spring tide. The tiny blue eggs are deposited in these burrows. Why do you think that the horseshoe crabs come ashore at spring tides to lay their eggs? (See Chapter Note 3 for a brief explanation.)

Over the next week or so, if you continue to observe very carefully in the same area, you may see the masses of developing eggs and perhaps even observe the tiny forms of the crabs as they mature. These egg masses are a major food source for many migrating shore birds.

How the Crabs Turn Over. Place a horseshoe crab in the sandy shallows. Gently turn the animal over so that its legs are up, facing the surface of the water. How does it turn itself back to a walking position? How long does it take? Do larger crabs take longer to turn over than smaller crabs? Do you think that this is an important survival skill? Explain your answer.

EXPLORATIONS

Rate of Speed, Old vs. Young. Horseshoe crabs begin their journey to protected beaches and mud flats in early spring, weeks prior to the breeding season. At this time it is generally easy to find them in the shallows of protected bays and coves. Select one and place it on the sand. Mark the spot where you set it down with a stone or similar object. After one minute, use a tape measure to determine the distance that the crab traveled from the stone. How far did your horseshoe crab travel in one minute? Find several other crabs of about the same size. How far does each of them travel in one minute? What is their average rate of speed on the sand? Try this with a sample of crabs that are smaller or larger than those in the first group. Does the size of the crab affect the rate of speed on sand? Do you think that the rate of speed would be different if the crabs were moving in the water instead of on the sand? Try it. The receding water often leaves shallow pools on the beach. Place the crab in one of these pools and observe its movements. Does it move sideways underwater? Does it move faster underwater than it does on land?

Squatters Are Everywhere. When you examine each of the horseshoe crabs, observe how many individuals in this population have growths of algae and barnacles on their shields. While you are observing, look for another interesting visitor. More formally known as *Bdelloura candida*, the horseshoe crab flatworm can be found attached to the undersurface of horseshoe crabs. Although generally white-beige in color, these interlopers may also be pale yellow. The worms are not parasites. Instead, they enjoy a commensal relationship with the crab, and this relationship is essential to the worm's life. Researchers have discovered that when removed from the horseshoe crab, the worms don't eat and soon die. Examine several horseshoe crabs. Look for these flatworms. Where do you find them and how many are there in each location? Do they seem to cluster in one or more places? Are they somewhat evenly distributed?

CHAPTER NOTES

1. The Range of *Limulus*. Although found from the Gulf of Maine to the Gulf of Mexico, alas, *Limulus* is not a visitor to the west coast. However, they can often be seen in commercial aquaria that feature animals from distant places.

2. The Feeding Legs. Shorter than the other legs, the feeding legs of the horseshoe crab grab pieces of food and pass them to the bristles that grow at the base of the next four pairs of legs, called walking legs. Particles of worms, mollusks, and algae are ground by the bristles and passed into the mouth, located between the third and fifth pairs of legs. This feeding system is designed so that the animal can eat only when on the move, literally shoveling food into its mouth.

3. The Spring Tides. There are approximately two weeks between the unusually high tides that come during the new and full phases of the lunar cycle. Horseshoe crabs bury their eggs in sand that is not touched by the tide for two weeks. The eggs develop in the warm, moist sand just below the surface. If they survive the probing beaks of the migrating shore birds, they hatch in two weeks and are washed back into the water by the second highest tide of the month.

CHAPTER 9

Eelgrass

SALTWATER MEADOWS

I love to take a solitary walk along the beach at any time of the year. The sound of the surf and the smell of the fresh breeze mixed with the smell of seaweed and sand are both restful and invigorating. Inevitably, I become fascinated by the little treasures that lie half hidden in the line of seaweeds, shells, straw, and sticks that meanders down the beach parallel to the water.

This line of debris, called the strand line, contains assorted refuse that has been "stranded" by falling tides or tossed on the beach by waves. Before long, I find myself collecting a hat full of empty mollusk shells, crab carapaces, whelk egg cases, smooth beach glass, and strange twisted bits of wood. As I turn over the debris, I wonder at the little creatures who live here, the springing, hopping, squirming amphipods who scurry away at my intrusion.

These strand lines also include a large variety of plant material. The species that you'll find are generally those that grow in local offshore waters, such as bright green sheets of sea lettuce (*Ulva*), long olive-brown blades from *Laminaria*, fleshy green fingers of *Codium*, and deep red tufts of Irish moss. Frequently, you will notice dark green or brown, ribbon-like leaves of eelgrass distributed in the litter. Since only the leaves of the eelgrass plant lie among the drying seaweeds, it's easy to dismiss these leaves as simply part of some seaweed or as a land grass that got washed into the sea.

Eelgrass, however, is not from dry land, nor is it a seaweed. It's a grass, and like all grasses, *Zostera marina* is a flowering plant. Unlike other grasses, eelgrass lives underwater in the shallows that extend beyond the low-tide line. This shallow water often lies behind an offshore sandbar; it provides a buffer zone between the shoreline and the open sea. Here, with a face mask and snorkel, you can explore a gentle, stable community that supports an abundance of life forms.

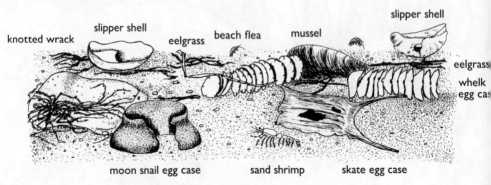

Strand line

Despite its watery environment, eelgrass is similar to the familiar grasses of a city park, a suburban lawn, or a field of barley. Like its land-based cousins, but unlike seaweeds, each underwater eelgrass plant has green leaves, stems, and roots. Even more remarkable, it produces small, inconspicuous flowers, complete with pollen and seeds. It does this in an underwater habitat that lacks wind, bees, and other mechanisms generally associated with successful plant reproduction.

Like its shore-bound grassy cousins, *Zostera marina* increases the size of its growth area by developing horizontal underground stems called rhizomes. New plants extend upward from the rhizomes, and roots grow down from them to anchor the plants in the soft, sandy mud. This sediment is the major reservoir for plant nutrients that are absorbed through the root systems. Some researchers, however, believe that eelgrass *leaves* can also extract some food material directly from the water itself. Nutrients may enter at the leaf surfaces in a way similar to that of the seaweeds. The land grasses cannot do anything like this. (See Chapter Note 1 for a discussion of *Zostera* leaves.)

The other reproductive strategy used by eelgrass in common with land grasses is sexual in nature, since it involves the fusion of male and female reproductive cells, or gametes. Stringy, gelatinous pollen is produced by the male portion of eelgrass flowers, the anther. The slimy pollen is then carried by water currents to the stigma of a female flower. There the pollen settles, fertilization occurs, and seeds are produced. By August the seeds are mature; from 50 to 250 seeds are released from each parent plant. Some seeds settle in the nutrient-rich sediment, and if conditions are satisfactory, they germinate, producing new plants. Other seeds remain on the parent plant. By late summer, these grasses die, and with the remaining seeds, the stems are carried by tidal currents to distant places to establish a new colony.

The extensive and effective network of eelgrass roots stabilizes bottom sediments and ultimately results in vast underground prairies of eelgrass in estuaries, coastal bays, and lagoons. The great mass of supple grass fronds, which sway rhythmically underwater in the passing currents, serves to dampen wave action, causing detritus particles to settle onto the mud surface. This detritus acts as a fertilizer for the grass roots. This soft soil with the special life forms attracted to it is called a deposit community; it is a habitat where many clams, worms, burrowing anemones, and other mud-loving animals make their homes. The bay scallop is an economically important mollusk that is found in the eelgrass deposit community.

The extensive eelgrass meadows also provide shelter and food for other plants and many kinds of animals, such as fish and crustaceans. Some of these plants and animals live permanently among the *Zostera* plants, while other organisms are more transient, only looking for a safe refuge or bed and breakfast. The long term results of the eelgrass presence is that the sediment buildup causes the water to become increasingly shallow until mud flats are exposed at low tide. At this point the eelgrass is replaced by *Spartina* grasses and a salt marsh begins to form.

One of the greatest contributions of eelgrass to the marine community is the additional surface area provided by its dense foliage, which supplies a habitat where epiphytic algae, such as the tiny green, red, and blue-green algae, can grow. Larger algal forms of seaweeds, such as the yellow-brown *Ectocarpus* and the green gut weeds, *Enteromorpha*, also find a place for attachment on *Zostera* leaf blades. With the addition of these chlorophyll-containing organisms, photosynthetic activity in an eelgrass community rises substantially.

There are countless numbers of invertebrates, such as amphipods, grass shrimps, New England dog whelks and other snails, tunicates, and various crabs and lobsters, that make their homes in the *Zostera* ecosystem. They graze on the panoply of epiphytic algae that grows profusely on the surface of the eelgrass leaves, or they prey upon grazing animals. Hordes of the sessile animals, such as sponges, coiled tube worms, and bryozoans, live attached to *Zostera* leaves. Included in the roll call of citizenry are fish species, such as mummichogs, Atlantic needlefish, sticklebacks, eels, silver perch, and summer flounder. The list of grazers, scavengers, deposit feeders, and filter feeders is also impressive. Biologists who have carried out extensive research in eelgrass communities report that every known phylum has a representative living there. Indeed, there is a rich diversity of life forms in this underwater world. Almost five million tons of eelgrass are eaten every year by ducks and geese. The total amount growing around the shores of the North Atlantic every year is estimated by scientists to be twenty-four million tons.

Beginning in 1931, the tremendous ecological and economic importance of eelgrass became apparent when *Zostera* fields along the Atlantic coast suffered an epidemic that resulted in a catastrophic decline in eelgrass. This die-off ended in 1933, but full recovery took another twenty years. The effects of the destruction of eelgrass on waterfowl, arthropod, mollusk, and fish populations were staggering. Many marine industries depend directly on eelgrass for fertilizer, fuel, garden mulch, packaging, home insulation, and soundproofing. Other industries, such as the scallop fishery and duck and goose hunting, depend indirectly on eelgrass. Scientists believe that the causes for this die-off were related to a warming trend during the summer months, which persisted for several years around 1931. In the excessive heat, eelgrass lost its vigor and became susceptible to invasions by fungi and bacteria. By 1933, the eelgrass began to recover, and finally, by 1951, *Zostera* had made a spectacular comeback in most regions along the coast.

This great eelgrass disaster is a warning for us. If man causes global heating, we now know what to expect in the shallow saltwater ecosystems of the North Atlantic. Certainly there will be similar widespread effects in every other ecosystem.

Another very important contribution of *Zostera* to a bay or estuary system comes at the death and subsequent decay of the plants. The remains of the *Zostera* are ultimately re-formed into detritus. Through these processes, eelgrass releases enormous amounts of nutrient-rich material into the surrounding waters. Tidal action then distributes this rich fertilizer.

The process of decay begins with the coming of cold weather, when there are tremendous changes in the *Zostera* habitat. Similar to other grasses, the plants die back in the fall, denuding the mud surface. Only the rhizomes and roots remain under the mud. Seasonal habitat destruction such as this causes a few of the animal members of the eelgrass community to die, their bodies becoming part of the detritus cycle. Some creatures migrate to the protection of deep water, while other animals crawl into the soft mud to a foul-weather haven. There they patiently wait for the tilt of the earth to bring back life-giving sunlight to their corner of the watery world.

THE WORLD OF EELGRASS

What you will need	Science skills
basic kit	*observing*
face mask	*recording*
snorkel	*mapping*
sieve	*inferring*
keen eyes	*comparing*

OBSERVATIONS

Locating Eelgrass. You are most likely to find eelgrass (*Zostera marina*) flourishing in the shoals of protected areas along the Atlantic coast from South Carolina to the Arctic and scattered along the length of the Pacific coast from Alaska to Mexico. *Zostera marina* also flourishes in the shallows of quiet embayments in the Gulf of Mexico. While fishing from a small boat in one of these protected bays or just rowing along the outer edges of a salt marsh, you may see the tips of eelgrass blades poking above the water's surface as they gently sway to the rhythm of the waves. Although you never find eelgrass in the crashing surf of the open ocean, you will frequently see it while swimming or wading a few yards offshore in quiet bays or coves. Since commercial shellfish, such as scallops, clams, and lobsters, make their homes in eelgrass meadows, local fishermen are often able to tell you where to find "a grassy bottom." (See Chapter Note 2 for a discussion of water depth and eelgrass.)

As you explore this fascinating habitat, you'll find that *Zostera* is the framework around which a very complex and highly productive community thrives. The ecological importance of this habitat will become apparent when you begin a survey of the plants and animals that live there and discover the niches these life forms fill.

Identifying Sea Grasses. Once you have found an area of sea grass in water shallow enough to investigate, your first task is to identify the grass. This will be easy, because there are only three common types along our eastern coast. In the north, *Zostera* is the most common type. Further south, along the mid-Atlantic coast south of Virginia, shoal grass, or *Halodule wirghtii*, grows in lush beds. It is also abundant in the Gulf of Mexico, where you can frequently find it exposed at low tide. The three-pointed blade tips of shoal grass distinguish it from its look-alike neighbor, eelgrass, which has single, rounded blade tips.

Another member of the sea grass group, often found growing by itself in luxuriant beds, is widgeon grass *(Ruppia maratina)*. This plant grows better in water that is less salty than that preferred by *Zostera*. You will find it in that portion of estuaries where fresh water enters the system through rivers and land runoff.

Which kind of sea plants have you found? Is there more than one variety in your area? What inferences can you make about the salinity of the water based on the presence of particular grasses?

Along the exposed rocky shores of the west coast from Alaska to Mexico, you'll find several species of surf grass *(Phyllospadix)*. The blades of this grass grow to six feet in length. The blades resemble eelgrass, but they are thinner. (See the suggested field guide to the Pacific coast listed in the Bibliography.)

Variations in Eelgrass. Eelgrass leaves are not always the same length or width. Eelgrass growing in sandy, shallow areas where the water is often churned up has short, narrow leaves. If it grows in deeper, quieter waters, eelgrass has longer, wider leaves. What are the conditions of the water in your study area? Is it turbid or clear? Which type of *Zostera* do you find?

Eelgrass and Sediment Buildup. In the sea grass community, do you find the plants widely spaced or are they growing close together? Are there clues that suggest how the plants affect wave action, water flow, and sediment

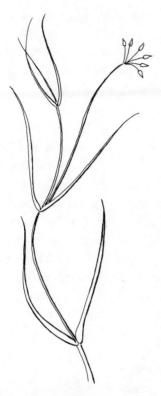

Widgeon grass (Ruppia Maritima)

buildup? Feel the bottom material between the plants. Is it soft and oozy? Compare this bottom material with that found nearby where there are no eelgrass plants. Spread out a few fistfuls of the eelgrass sediment on a sheet of plastic. What do you find? If you wash it through your sieve, you may find some interesting material to examine with your hand lens.

Eelgrass and the Seaweeds. Are there any large seaweeds, such as *Fucus*, *Ascophyllum*, or *Laminaria* (kelp), growing in the area? (See Chapter Note 3 for an explanation of this relationship.) In some eelgrass beds, each blade of grass seems to have an unusually large diameter, often up to about two inches across. When you feel these grass blades, you realize that the actual blade is of normal size, but it is surrounded by a mass of greenish brown fuzz. Remove one of these blades and examine it. The fuzz seems to disappear. Where do you think the fuzz went? Examine it with your hand lens. Remove a blade of eelgrass that seems to be free of algae and gently rub it between your fingers. How does it feel? Examine the grass blade with a hand lens. The fuzz you see and the slipperiness you feel is due to tiny algae plants that live on the eelgrass. Algae that live in this way are called epiphytes, which literally means "living on the surface of a plant." The algae "guests" that you find growing on the eelgrass "host" are probably species of *Polysiphonia*, *Ceramium*, *Cladophora*, or *Entero-morpha*, depending on the geographical region in which the eelgrass is grow-ing. The epiphytes you find in eelgrass communities of Long Island Sound could be quite different from those you discover living in more southerly waters.

Eelgrass and Ducks. Do you see Canada geese or Brant geese feeding on eelgrass beds? Do you see any ducks feeding? Some ducks feed by pivoting on the surface with their head, neck, and forward body submerged. These are called dabbling ducks. Mallards, common teals, gadwalls, and northern pintails are all dabbling ducks that you might observe dipping for food in the eelgrass community. You might see some ducks that dive completely out of sight in the eelgrass beds. Not surprisingly, these are called diving ducks. Canvasbacks and redheads are diving ducks that you might see. Don't forget to check your regional field guides for local species. As you progress through the explora-tions, you will develop a good idea of what each sort of duck might be eating in the eelgrass beds. How has natural selection designed these two groups of ducks so that they are not competing for the same food source? (See Chapter Note 4 for a brief note on duck feeding.)

EXPLORATIONS

Exploring the Eelgrass Community. Animal life flourishes in an eelgrass community. As you swim slowly over the underwater meadow, using snorkel and mask, you will begin to find creatures of all sizes and shapes. Some of the animals you find will be very mobile, freely swimming among the blades of grass, while others roam very little around the community or may be firmly anchored to the eelgrass. Other groups of life forms live in or on the soft sediment. The explorations that follow will help you organize the great diver-sity of life forms that you will find.

Eelgrass Climbers. One group of animals includes all those that graze on the blades of eelgrass. Some members of this group are convex slipper limpets (*Crepidula convexa*), periwinkles, mud snails, and glass shrimps. You might also see the animals that prey upon these grazers, such as oyster drills and dog whelks. Varieties of ribbon worms, clam worms, and flatworms also find food to their liking on eelgrass. See if you can find some of these and add them to your list of community members.

Life in the Sediment. The sediment in the eelgrass community provides shelter for other groups of animals. Some of these beasts live on the sandy mud, while others prefer to make their living while buried in the soft muck. Look for surface dwellers, such as mussels and scallops. To uncover the in-

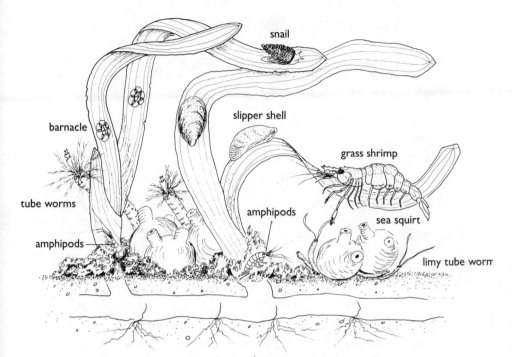

Eelgrass community (not to scale)

dwellers, gently dig up some of the silt with a small trowel. Put this material into a bucket or other suitable container. When you return to your boat, put the sediment into a sieve and flush some seawater through it. What animals do you find living in the muck? (See Chapter Note 5 for a brief roll call of the mud dwellers.)

Other Eelgrass Epiphytes. Eelgrass blades provide a foundation for many other tiny life forms. Remove some blades of eelgrass and examine them carefully with your hand lens. Using your field guide for assistance, see if you can identify some of the following: sea squirts, hydroids, transparent egg capsules, or sedentary polychaetes, such as *Spirobis*, sponges, or bryozoans. Make a separate list of these animals. The chart that follows will help you group the variety of living things you find, according to one of their roles in the community.

Mapping the Sequence of Life on Eelgrass. Make a "larger-than-life" drawing of one eelgrass blade. As you find different plant and animal life forms on the eelgrass, mark your drawing with the location of that living guest of the eelgrass. As you continue your explorations you will develop a "map" showing the sequence of life.

Marine biologists say that an eelgrass community is a miniature version of

A SURVEY OF AN EELGRASS COMMUNITY

Community Members	Name of Life Form(s)	Number
Epiphytes		
1. Algae		
2. Beasts		
Grazers		
Sediment dwellers		
Free swimmers		

Location:

Date:

Weather Conditions:

a "piling" community. The wooden pilings of docks and bulkheads contain the same kinds of animals that you found on eelgrass. Furthermore, the animals occupy relatively similar positions on the blades of grass as they do on the wooden pilings. Find a piling that is host to marine life, and see if you can find those animals you discovered in the eelgrass community. Make a sketch of your piling, and indicate on your drawing, or "map," where you found living things. Compare this map with the map of your eelgrass blade. How are the two sequences alike or how are they different?

Food Chains and Food Webs in the Eelgrass Community. As you have discovered, *Zostera* meadows provide shelter for an impressive list of larger animals. Needlefish, sticklebacks, flounder, silver perch, spotfish, and various species of crabs and shrimps are only a few of the larger species of sea life that make their homes among the eelgrass blades. Find some of these animals and see if you can discover their niche in the community. Based on your observations, make a diagram of several food chains. Using your food chains, make an eelgrass community food web. Don't forget to include the dipping ducks, the geese, and us. Indicate the energy flow through the food web.

CHAPTER NOTES

1. The Roots and Leaves of Eelgrass. *Zostera* has a shallow root system and a broad, flat leaf for absorbing nutrients directly from the water. If you inspect a *Zostera* leaf through a microscope, you will not find any stomata, those microscopic holes on the undersurface of the leaf through which carbon dioxide and oxygen are exchanged in the process of photosynthesis. *Zostera* carries out this exchange through the leaf cells.

2. Water Depth and Eelgrass Growth. Eelgrass grows at an average depth of about nine or ten feet below the water's surface. This means that some eelgrass grows in deeper water and some grows in more shallow water. The tidal range must also be considered, because the eelgrass will not grow in an area where it would be regularly exposed at low tide. At most, you will only find the very tips of the eelgrass showing above the surface of the water. Is this consistent with what you found?

3. Seaweeds in the Eelgrass Beds. The holdfasts of macroalgae, or seaweeds, cannot grab hold in the soft, sandy mud, so you will not find them growing directly in the sediment. However, since there are generally rocks or small stones in the eelgrass beds, the holdfasts can anchor the seaweeds to these substrates, so you may find some seaweeds in the community.

4. Ducks in the Eelgrass. You often see large numbers of ducks feeding in a small, quiet cove. On closer inspection, you may find that there are several different species of ducks. How can this cove support so many different kinds of ducks? Through natural selection, many different feeding strategies have evolved. Various species of ducks can coexist, because they fill different niches. As far as nutrients are concerned, this means that since they have different food sources, they can avoid competition.

5. Eelgrass Sediment. Research tells us, and your own observations will confirm the fact, that the muddy sediment of eelgrass communities is rich with life. This includes clams, burrowing anemones, sand shrimps, a variety of polychaetes, and a tremendous assortment of amphipods and isopods.

CHAPTER 10

Fish

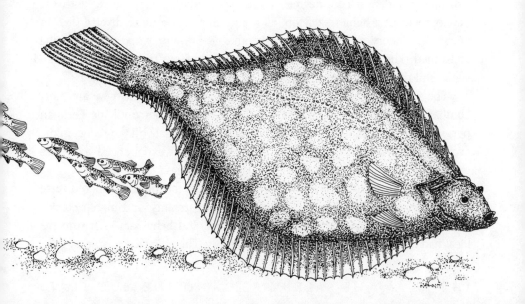

A LONG STORY OF CHANGE

About 450 million years ago, the earth was covered by warm, shallow seas, which were home to countless tribes of strange invertebrates, such as trilobites and other crustaceans that fed on the great abundance of tiny algae. During that period of the earth's history, jawless fish thrived in the waters. Lacking the more advanced fin system of their descendants, jawless fish were not good swimmers. These slow-moving filter feeders supped primarily on plankton, which drifted freely in the surrounding waters. Although the golden age of jawless fish lasted for about 150 million years, this ancestral line is represented today by only about fifty species of long, slender, eel-shaped lampreys and hagfish.

In the course of the earth's violent geological history, the landscape and seascape changed radically. The seabed dropped and was reorganized into deep oceanic trenches, while rift valleys were chiseled into the ocean floor. Streams and rivers coursed seaward from their sources in mountain watersheds high above the sea, bringing sediment and mineral matter into the oceans. The newer waters were deeper, colder, and chemically different, not a proper home for jawless fish, which remained confined to the shallows. Therefore, the deep water continued to be uninhabited until life forms could adapt to the new conditions and exploit these pristine environments.

During the next 100 million years, the Devonian period of earth history, two significant events occurred in the fish world. One of these was the appearance of fish with jaws and teeth, which made them capable of grabbing and tearing. The other significant change was the development of paired fins. This modification corrected the lurching and swiveling swimming style of earlier fish and provided a new degree of stability. These changes, along with the development of a lighter skeleton, allowed fish to eat a more diverse diet, to become predatory, and to swim faster both to capture prey and to avoid being consumed. The early fish, although not exactly like our modern fish, were so successful that the Devonian period is referred to as the "Age of Fishes."

The spectacularly successful, modern bony fish with which we are most familiar didn't develop for another 100 million years, not until the Permian period 280 to 230 million years ago. Although arriving late on the scene, in the evolutionary sense, those fish and their descendants experienced a species explosion unknown in any other group of living things.

Today, bony fish can be found from the Arctic to the tropics in such diverse habitats as the open ocean, tide pools, brackish streams, and marsh creeks. They come in contrasting sizes, shapes, colors, and behaviors. A trip to the local fish market will reveal some of this variety. There you'll see, side by side, the streamlined torpedo shape of the fast swimming mackerel and wahoo contrasting with the slower moving, flat, pan-shaped flounder, halibut, and sole. Natural selection has worked to design the shape of flatfish, whose survival is not dependent on speed, but rather on their ability to change color so that they blend with the sandy bottom where they live.

Much of our literature about the sea is romanticized, but life in the watery environment is not always rosy. Changes in temperature, salinity, and pressure and low light levels in the sea have resulted in the evolution of specialized sensory and respiratory organs to cope with difficult conditions. Fish have also developed provisions for movement and buoyancy within their special environment.

Let's take a look at some of the more unusual adjustments made by those very successful vertebrates, the bony fish. Fish hear well. Researchers have learned that many fish, although lacking external ears, have specially designed auditory receptors that pass sound vibrations to fluid-filled tubes of the inner ear. These canals are equipped with tiny hairs, or cilia, which transmit sound impulses through a series of complex mechanical and chemical actions to the fish's brain for processing. Ear stones, or otoliths, part of the auditory system, are associated with sensory cells and are important aids in the auditory/balance mechanisms of the bony fish. Otoliths are valuable to scientists, who use them to identify fish species. They can also use otoliths to determine the age of a fish, because, as the fish grows, the otolith develops concentric, annual rings. Scientists count these rings with the aid of a microscope.

Fish also have another sensory perception system, called the lateral line system. This system is unique to fish and has no equivalent in any other vertebrate group. The lateral line system enables fish to detect low frequency vibrations, turbulence, and pressure changes, such as those made by a passing

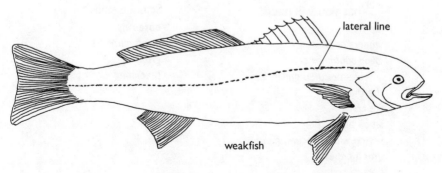

Typical shape and position of the lateral line

creature or the plunk of a fisherman's lure. Vibrations from the watery environment pass through pores in the body scales and are channeled to sensory receptors on the lateral line system. Fish researchers think that the lateral line is also responsible for keeping schools of fish together. The line runs more or less horizontally from behind the gills to the tail and can be seen along the sides of the body in many fish species.

A third organ associated with hearing and balance is the swim bladder, an air-filled sac located below the backbone in bony fish. Except for bottom dwellers, such as sculpins and catfish, for whom a buoyancy organ does not provide selective advantage, most bony fish have well-developed air bladders. Evolved from the lungs of primitive Devonian fish, this air-filled sac is a very efficient flotation device. By adjusting the volume of gas in the swim bladder, a fish can regulate its depth in the water. Through a network of capillaries, oxygen and some other gases, such as carbon dioxide, nitrogen, and carbon monoxide, are transferred to the gas bladder from the circulating blood. The direction of gas flow depends on whether the fish needs to increase its buoyancy and float toward the surface of the water or reduce its buoyancy and go deeper.

Fishermen who use bait rather than lures tell us that fish have an excellent sense of smell. Scientists have verified this, finding that, with the aid of chemical receptors located in special sacs in the nostrils, fish can detect extremely small amounts of some substances in the water. Taste in water is also achieved by chemical receptors. Specialized "taste buds" are located on the skin, lips, and fins of fish. These are just some of the adaptations that fish have developed throughout evolutionary time and that have placed them among the most beautifully designed creatures on our watery planet.

THE WORLD OF FISH

What you will need	Science skills
dip net	observing
waders or boots	using numbers
clear container or	graphing
wide-mouthed gallon jar	predicting
thermometer	
ice chips	
small plastic bag	
watch with a second hand	
graph paper	
persistence	

OBSERVATIONS

Maintaining a Live Fish. Although you have looked at various fish many times, systematic observation is a very different way of seeing. A good way to begin systematic observation is to capture one of the small fish that inhabit the intertidal area and observe its structure and its behavior. It would be better for you to catch two or three fish, each of a different species. Three-spined sticklebacks and killies can be scooped up with a dip net as they swim in salt marsh tidal creeks or in a bed of eelgrass. If the water is warm, you will be comfortable wearing an old pair of sneakers; otherwise you might want to wear a pair of waders or high rubber boots. If you want to cheat a little, you can get your fish from someone selling "live bait."

After obtaining your fish, put them into a clear container large enough for them to swim freely. A wide-mouthed gallon jar usually works well for two or three small fish. Resist the temptation to add more than three small fish to a one-gallon container unless you use an air pump. Add water from their natural habitat until the container is about three-quarters full. *Do not use tap water.* Keep the container in a bright, sunny area, so that the algae in the water remain alive, but not in direct sunlight, which might cook the fish. Even though this is only a temporary holding tank for your fish, you could add some seaweed, which will supply oxygen to your system.

Recording the Details of Fish Structure. The best way to concentrate on the important variations in fish structure is to sketch the details in a systematic way. Artistic quality is not important; accuracy is the goal. Start with one fish and then perhaps do others. Begin with the discussion of body shape and then go on to the other topics.

YOUR FISH ILLUSTRATION

General Body Shape: Fish come in a variety of shapes. The torpedo-shaped fish are streamlined for high speed. Although fish with this shape, like the skipjack tuna, are swift swimmers, they lack maneuverability. Fully grown, rapid swimmers such as these would not be found hunting prey among the blades of eelgrass; they would pursue their food in the open ocean where fine, delicate movements are unnecessary.

Fish whose bodies are compressed, as if they were squeezed from right to left, lack the ability to swim fast, but they are extremely agile and can thread their way among the rocks to feed. Examples of fish with this body style are the lookdown along the east coast and the crevalle jack, a Pacific coast swimmer.

Flat-bodied fish, such as flounder, sole, and halibut, are designed for life on

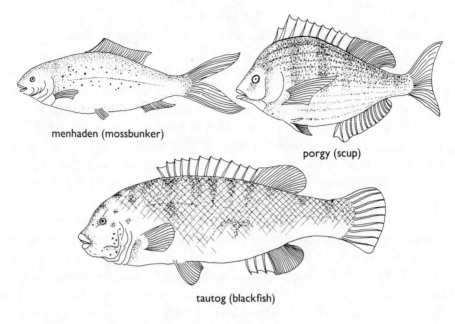

menhaden (mossbunker)

porgy (scup)

tautog (blackfish)

Variations in fish shapes

a soft and malleable bottom. With the prying action of their dorsal fins, flatfish such as these can bury themselves in sand or mud to escape their predators. Although flatfish are not long-distance travelers, they can lunge with speed and accuracy. Begin your fish diagram with the body shape, ignoring details of the fins and tail.

Shape and Location of Fins: How many fins does your fish have on the top surface of its body? Where are they located? These are the dorsal fins. Now observe the bottom fins (the pelvic fins and the anal fin). Next look at the fins on the sides of the body. These provide balance. Are any of the fins in pairs? Where do you find them? In the drawing, sketch in the fins as they appear on your fish. How do the fins on your fish compare with those in the drawing in Chapter Note 1? If you're lucky enough to have a three-spined stickleback in your container, you'll see that the dorsal fins have been reduced to a few disconnected spines. What happens to the spines when you touch them? Does the dorsal fin extend the length of the fish body; is it continuous? If not, how many dorsal fins are there? Two? Three? Are the fins spiny or soft? Or are they both? The tail is also a fin, the caudal fin. Note the shape of the tail. Is it forked, rounded, square? (See Chapter Note 2 for a detailed description of the locations and functions of fins.)

The Lateral Line: Look for a line on the side of the fish. It is called the lateral

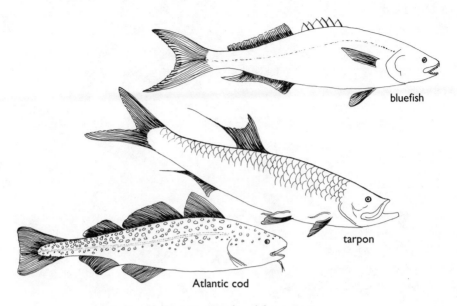

Variations in dorsal fins

line and varies from one species of fish to another. Is it a thin black line that extends to the end of the tail, as in the snook, an Atlantic sport fish? Is the line a pale color, as in the white hake? Does the line make a gentle arch as it passes over the pectoral fins, as in the white perch of the Atlantic or as in the Pacific coast yellowtail? What other variations in the lateral line can you find? Add the lateral line to your sketch if you observe one.

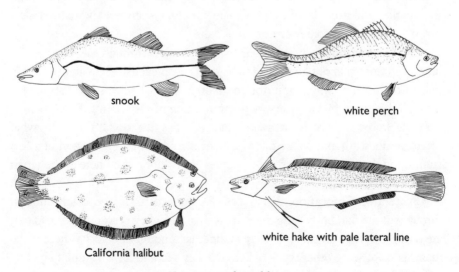

Variations in lateral lines

FISH

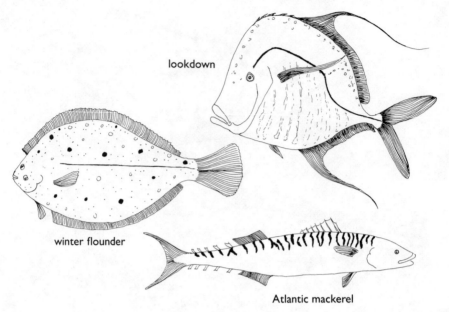

lookdown

winter flounder

Atlantic mackerel

Variations in tail fins

Other Fish Details: At this point, you have observed the basic structural features of a fish. Other details, such as coloration, the shape of the head, and the location of the eyes, mouth, and gills, can now be added to your sketch.

Visit some commercial fishing boats that have returned from a morning's work. How many different kinds of body shapes, fin locations, and tail shapes can you find among their catch? If you cannot meet the commercial boats, a fish market will provide you with similar variety. Fishermen and fish retailers can often show you some very unusual fish.

Fish Locomotion. Observe your fish as it swims through the water. If you have been unable to obtain a small fish, go to a tropical fish shop and observe a fish in one of the tanks. Describe the motion of its body as the fish swims through the water. Make observations from different viewpoints. Does the fish keep its body straight as it swims along? Does the body bend? In what direction does it bend? Write a few sentences to describe the motion of a fish swimming through the water. (See Chapter Note 3 for a brief note on how fish swim.)

Protective Coloration. What color is your fish? Is the color uniform throughout the fish body? Are there areas that are light in color and others that are darker? Where on the fish body is the least amount of color? Where is the most? Look at some other types of fish. Do they seem to have a similar shading pattern? Light in one area and dark in another? What advantage do you think this pattern of coloration or shading is to the fish? (See Chapter Note 4 for a brief explanation of this kind of protective coloration.)

Fish Slime. A close examination of a freshly caught fish will give you some more information about these highly successful vertebrates. Rub your hand back and forth over the fish body. How does it feel? Dry or slimy? The slipperiness is due to a film of mucus, secreted by special glands, which helps the fish move smoothly through the water. The film also protects the fish from disease bacteria. For these reasons, it's not a good idea to handle live fish for more than a few seconds, since you might remove some of this very important material.

Fish Scales. While you still have a larger fish in hand, note the scales that cover the fish. In what direction do they grow? Run your hand along the fish body from the tail end to the head. How does it feel? Run your hand along the fish body in the opposite direction. What difference did you notice? What is the advantage for the fish to have scales pointing toward its tail? Birds that feed on whole fish never swallow the fish tail first; instead, the meal goes down headfirst. Why do you think this is so?

You can find many fish scales anywhere fish are cleaned or handled. Gather up a few. Look at the edges of the scales with a hand lens. What do they look like? Are the edges of the scales smooth and curved, or are they comb-like with teeth? (See Chapter Note 5 for the "scoop" on scales.)

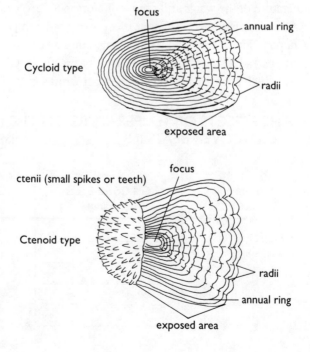

Fish scales

EXPLORATIONS

The Effects of Water Temperature. In making observations of the fish you caught, you probably have noticed the rhythmic opening and closing of your fish's mouth and gills. What is the relationship between the beat of the fish's mouth and that of the gill covers, located behind its eyes?

Is there a relationship between the temperature of the water and the rhythmic beats of the gill covers? To find out, put your fish into a container of seawater. Take the temperature of the water and record it on a chart similar to the one below. Now count the number of gill-cover beats in one minute. (To shorten the procedure, count the gill-cover beats for fifteen seconds and multiply that number by four.) Record the number of gill-cover beats. The next step is to lower the temperature of the water. You can do this without diluting the saltwater by adding ice chips that are sealed in a small plastic bag. Drop this package into the water and wait for two minutes. Take the temperature again and record it. Count the number of gill-cover beats at this temperature. As the water continues to cool, repeat the procedure at two-minute intervals. This will not harm the fish.

To have a better display of the relationship between water temperature and gill-cover beats, put your data on a graph like the one on the next page. What would you predict the rate of gill-cover beats would be at the next lower temperature? Try it. What did you find out about the relationship between the temperature of the water and the respiratory rate in your fish?

A Look at Fish Gills. The four nostrils on your fish (see the fish illustration in Chapter Note 1) are used for smelling, but they do not function as breathing organs. Instead, fish use their gill system for breathing. Gills are made up of gill arches, which support gill rakers. These structures trap minute particles in the

THE EFFECTS OF TEMPERATURE ON THE NUMBER OF GILL-COVER BEATS IN _____ (FISH SPECIES)

Water, Degrees F	Gill-Cover Beats per Minute	Average Number of Gill-Cover Beats/ Temperature
70°	___ , ___ , ___ , ___	
65°	___ , ___ , ___ , ___	
60°	___ , ___ , ___ , ___	
55°	___ , ___ , ___ , ___	
50°	___ , ___ , ___ , ___	

THE EFFECTS OF TEMPERATURE ON GILL-COVER BEATS

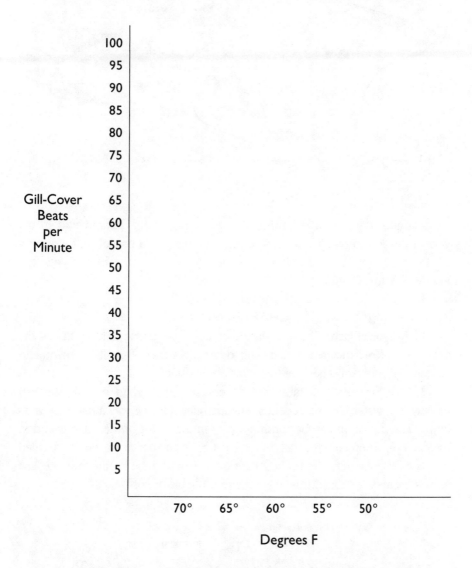

water that might damage the delicate gill filaments. It's across these filaments that oxygen passes into the blood of the fish and carbon dioxide is removed from the circulating blood.

To get a good view of the gills, you can use a fish from the market or a fish head you have obtained from a fisherman. First you should remove the opercula, or gill covers. (Salmon heads are particularly useful for this.) Find the gills and the gill arches. What color are they? How do they feel? Bony fish have four

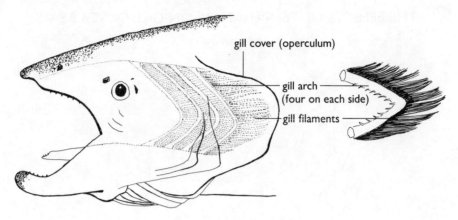

Gill structure of a bony fish

pairs of gills, while sharks have as many as seven pairs. Toxic metals in the water cause the protective mucus secreted by the gill to coagulate, disrupting gill function. Iron, for example, covers the gills with a dense brown coat that interferes with respiration.

CHAPTER NOTES

1. **A Typical Fish.** The following diagram of a generic fish illustrates the specialized fins, the lateral line, and other structures. It will be helpful to consult the diagram when making your observations

2. **Fish Fins.** As you have already noticed, fins aid in moving the fish through the water. Their size and shape are related to the way a fish makes its living. The dorsal fin can be continuous, as in the tautog of the Atlantic and in the opaleye, a popular gamefish of the Pacific. Or the dorsal fin can be divided into two or three parts, as in the Atlantic bluefish and the Pacific tomcod. The spines, or rays, in dorsal fins may be either pliable or stiff.

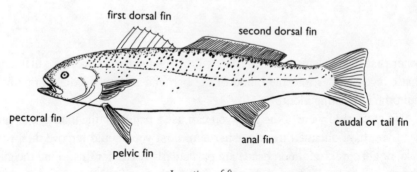

Location of fins

With the aid of the anal fin, dorsal fins act as a rudder and prevent the fish from rolling as it moves through the water. In some species of fish, the dorsal fins fold down. This enhances streamlining, an advantage for fast swimming.

Pectoral fins, found behind the gills, have several functions, depending on the type of fish. In general, pectoral fins help the fish glide, swim, and steer through the water. They are concerned with positioning and balancing a fish in the water column. Some fast swimmers are able to pull the pectoral fins close against their bodies. Other swift swimmers are equipped with depressions into which pectoral fins can fold. These adaptations effectively reduce drag as the fish glides through the water.

A pair of pelvic fins is below the pectoral fins. These fins can be found down from the gill cover or far back on the body, as in the Atlantic needlefish. They help the fish stay upright in the water.

Tail, or caudal, fins come in a variety of shapes. Porgies sport a forked tail, while the mummichog tail is rounded. Still another variation can be found in the squared-off tail of the sheepshead minnow. You can find these small fishes in tidal marsh creeks from the Gulf of St. Lawrence to northern Florida and the Gulf of Mexico. Similar variations can be seen in the forked tail of the California grunion. This little fish also sports a very long anal fin and two dorsal fins. You can expect to find it from the waters of San Francisco Bay to Baja California.

Lastly, fish have anal fins to keep them upright while swimming through the water. Like other fins, anal fins vary in shape and size. In fish that bear live young (as opposed to egg-laying fish), the anal fin has been modified to internally fertilize eggs.

3. How Fish Swim. When the fish swims, a wave of muscle contraction flows from head to tail and produces the thrust that propels the fish forward through the water. The next time you skin a freshly caught fish prior to eating it, look for the wavy bands of flesh that extend from the backbone of the fish to its belly (dorsal to ventral). The alternating contraction and relaxation of these muscles produce the characteristic S wave of the body of a swimming fish. To see this S wave, look down on the swimming fish from above.

4. Camouflage. Countershading is an important part of fish camouflage. The light coloring along the bottom of a fish makes it difficult for a predator, looking toward the surface of the water, to see its prey hovering in the water above. Similarly, looking down through the water column, it is equally difficult to see the dark dorsal surface of a fish against the dark bottom background. This shading also hides the fish in a side view by reversing the normal shadow pattern of a three-dimensional object. You may have experienced the way this countershading benefits the fish when you tried to find one to scoop up with your dip net. The movement of the fish may have been your first clue that it was close to you.

5. Scales. Another characteristic that separates fish from other vertebrates is the scales that cover the bodies of most fish species. Scales are modified skin cells. Their number does not change as the fish gets bigger. Instead, scales grow throughout the life of the fish. Each year of the fish's life, annual rings become recognizable on each scale. The rate of growth is determined by the availability of food, so it's not a surprise to find that fish grow faster in the summer and slower in the winter. This pattern of growth is reflected in the width of the growth rings.

There are several different types of scales found on bony fish. Spiny, comblike scales, or ctenoids, found on striped bass and mackerels are in contrast to the nonspiny, or cycloid, scales of cods. Illustrations of the two types of scales can be found on page 111.

CHAPTER 11

Marsh Plants

SALTY SURVIVORS

Spring has come to the tidal marsh. With the gradual warming of the soil, rhizomes, the underground stems of the marsh grasses, have begun producing enzymes. These chemical messengers trigger a series of cell divisions that will eventually produce new plants. Some of last year's crop produced seeds, as well. Those seeds not found by hungry birds and rodents during the winter and not washed away by winter storms have begun germinating. Soon tender, green stems will rise above the soil surface and begin sprouting leaves, which will make food for the young plants. Suddenly, the dead, brown stubble, the remains of last year's growth, gives way to the delicate, pale green of new life. The marsh awakens. Fresh growth is everywhere.

Salt marshes are communities of true plants. This means that the plants that thrive in them are land plants with special adaptations to survive in the marine environment. These special habitats, found flourishing along the edges of protected coves and bays, are unique to the temperate and polar latitudes. Some physical factors essential for the formation of salt marshes include gradual intertidal slopes, sediment deposits, protection from all but the gentlest wave action, and temperatures that fall below the freezing point for some part of the year.

When you visit the marsh, you will be impressed with the pattern of discrete zones of vegetation that exist there, each zone containing its own specific plant types. Elsewhere in nature, life is similarly organized into zones, but there is no place where the zones are more exquisitely laid out or more clearly defined than in the tidal marsh. A close look reveals that the arrangement of plants is not haphazard or random. It also becomes evident to the marsh plant detective that there is no plant species that grows everywhere in the tidal marsh. Each has its own special territory.

The slope of the land generally determines the width of the zones, and regardless of the size of the marsh, there is a meandering line that separates the low marsh from the high marsh. This boundary lies back from the shoreline and from the edges of the twisting tidal creeks and watercourses. It occurs at the level of the average height of high tide. In the eastern tidal marshes, this line separates the taller cordgrass, *Spartina alterniflora*, which grows near the water, from the shorter salt hay, *Spartina patens*, which grows on the landward side of the high-tide line. (In the western tidal marshes, *Spartina foliosa* grows near the water.)

The reasons for these growth patterns can be found in the special biological adaptations that have evolved in plants that live best either above or below the high-tide mark. In addition, in the area above the high-tide mark, various physical factors, such as wetness, salinity, and soil type, influence the type of plant that will grow. In the low marsh and along tidal creeks, *Spartina alterniflora* reigns supreme. Growing to a height of four to seven feet, *Spartina alterniflora* has no competition for its position in the marsh and clearly marks off the high-tide line by its height and color. It grows where it does because it is the only plant of the marsh that can tolerate regular tidal flooding for several hours each day.

Spartina cynosuroides is a common Gulf coast plant that grows well in slightly salted water, so you could expect to find this *Spartina* family member in brackish areas of the marsh. Its height of twelve feet or more helps to distinguish it from its genus mates *Spartina alterniflora* and *Spartina patens*.

Some slick detective work by plant scientists has unearthed several startling facts about *Spartina alterniflora*. To their surprise, they found that it is able to grow very well throughout the entire marsh, regardless of elevation, soil type, wetness, or salinity. They found that, like all other plants, it actually grows best under the freshwater conditions of the high marsh. However, in this ideal situation, it is eliminated by the other plants. The big survival advantage *Spartina alterniflora* has is the ability to also survive in a saltwater environment, which kills the other plants. If plants could have an attitude, the attitude of *Spartina alterniflora* would be, "Why fight the crowd when you can have the salty lowland all to yourself?"

Along the high-tide line of demarcation, which separates the low marsh from the high marsh, there is no overlapping of vegetation, nor is there any encroachment of *Spartina alterniflora* into the high-marsh territory of *Spartina patens*, or salt marsh hay. *Spartina patens* effectively keeps out the alterniflora by producing a dense network of underground stems and root mats. This prevents the new shoots of cordgrass from growing above the high-marsh mud. It also effectively prevents germinating seeds of *Spartina alterniflora* from taking root and establishing seedlings in the high marsh.

Although *Spartina patens* is clearly the leading lady of the high marsh, as you approach the landward border of the marsh, you will see that competition grows keen. *Juncus gerardi*, or black grass, another marsh perennial and a member of the rush family, often dominates the landward border of the marsh. This region of the tidal marsh is touched only when storm surges coincide with the highest of the high tides.

The primary reason that *Juncus gerardi* dominates over patens on the high border area of the marsh is because black grass begins its growth early in March and gets the jump on salt hay (*Spartina patens*), which begins its growth in May. This early start and a rapid growth rate give *Juncus* a competitive edge

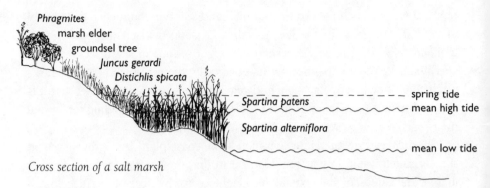

Spring tide

mean high tide

mean low tide

Phragmites
marsh elder
groundsel tree
Juncus gerardi
Distichlis spicata
Spartina patens
Spartina alterniflora

Cross section of a salt marsh

in establishing a foothold. Black grass does not encroach on the lower reaches of *Spartina patens* territory, because it is unable to survive the mats of seaweed brought by the spring tides. The seaweed becomes entangled around the bases of the patens plants. Thus, the tide protects salt hay from its competitor black grass by bringing seaweed into part of the marsh. The common name of *Juncus gerardi*, "black grass," comes from the very dark green (almost black) fruits that develop in June and remain until autumn.

A relative, *Juncus roemerianus*, is a very important member of the Gulf coast marsh community. It is a prolific rush, which occupies a great deal of space in the mid-littoral marsh zone. Other members of the *Juncus* clan can be found in many of the west coast marshes.

Another grass that has been studied by marsh plant investigators is spike grass, or *Distichlis spicata*. As its name implies, it is a very stiff plant. Spike grass is often confused with salt marsh hay, which it resembles in color and growth pattern. Its tousled appearance helps to distinguish it from *Spartina patens*. *Distichlis spicata* grows scattered throughout the high marsh in sandy soil.

A transitional area, which supports its own community of plants, lies beyond the upper limit of the *Spartina patens* zone in east coast marshes. Although usually associated with drier woodlands, the familiar, shiny green "leaves of three" that belong to poison ivy thrive here. The groundsel tree, or sea myrtle (*Baccharis halimifolia*), is also found along the upper edge of the marsh. The salt marshes from Maine to Georgia are home to this attractive shrub, which grows from three to nine feet tall. Its lovely yellow and white flowers add a delicate flavor to the marsh landscape from late summer through October.

Another east coast marsh shrub, which also grows to a height of three to nine feet, is the marsh elder (*Iva frutescens*). Since it is salt tolerant, marsh elder can invade the upper reaches of the *Spartina patens* zone, which lies just seaward of it. Its hairy leaves and stems help reduce water loss through evaporation. Frequently you'll see marsh elder standing tall in a *Spartina patens* prairie.

A discussion of the upland transition zone would not be complete without mention of *Phragmites communis*. These tall, picturesque reeds, growing in dense stands, form a backdrop for many of our tidal marshes. Although the ground around the tall stems is well-known for providing nesting sites for glossy ibis and black crowned night herons, the value of the reeds as a food source for wildlife is still being debated.

Probably the greatest liability of phragmites lies in its aggressive growth pattern, which outcompetes the more beneficial plants, such as the spartinas. When you see phragmites, you know that they mark an area where man has meddled with the marsh. The original salt marshes were not home to phragmites.

Salt marshes along the Pacific coast are not as extensive or as numerous as they are on the Atlantic coast. However, in spite of some climatic differences, many of the plants growing in these marsh systems are similar. When you visit

Common reed grass (Phragmites communis)

the Pacific marshes, you will find *Juncus* (black grass) growing along the edges of the high marsh, but the species of *Juncus* will change as you go from the west coast of Alaska to southern California. Similarly, you can find bulrushes (*Scirpus* sp.) growing in marshes from Point Barrow, Alaska, to lower California. Spike grass (*Distichlis spicata*) is found in drier sections of these marshes.

Spartina alterniflora has been introduced in a few places on the west coast, but *Spartina patens* is not found there at all. Instead of patens, *Spartina foliosa*, another introduced species, can often be found on the lower marsh. It is most abundant in the marshes of the San Francisco Bay area and diminishes in abundance southward.

Like the *Spartina* species on the east coast, the *Salicornia* species is probably the most important marsh plant in west coast marshes. As an example, *Salicornia* makes up almost 95 percent of the marsh vegetation in the San Francisco area and about 55 percent of the plant life of the lower marsh. It is probably the most important plant of the west coast marshes south of British Columbia.

In many places along our coast, the marshes that we see today are pitifully small remnants of the great, nutrient-rich marshes that once bordered our bays and sounds. Over 70 percent of the marshes along the heavily populated coast between New York and Boston have fallen victim to man's urge to "develop" the land. Nevertheless, the marshes that remain are places of rare beauty. One of the natural wonders of North America is the great marshlands of Georgia and the Carolinas, which stretch for miles between the mainland and the sea islands and barrier beaches.

THE WORLD OF MARSH PLANTS

What you will need
basic kit

Science skills
observing
measuring
comparing
identifying

OBSERVATIONS

A Good Way to Begin. The very best way to learn about any unfamiliar habitat is to visit that habitat with an expert guide. This is especially true of the salt marsh. All along the coasts of North America there are many nature centers that welcome visitors and provide guided tours of salt marshes. Many shore communities have a museum with seaside habitat exhibits. The local

Audubon Society chapter often sponsors habitat tours. You can find out about guided tours from the Chamber of Commerce or the Visitors' Bureau.

Cautions on Entering the Salt Marsh. The salt marsh is home to many plants and animals. It is also a special place where many different species of animals come to mate and raise their young. Disturbing the animals at this critical period in their life cycle could have disastrous results. A careless tide marsh stroller can frighten nesting birds and crush unhatched eggs. Another danger is trampling algae and seed plants that are delicate and sensitive to disturbance. Intrude into the marsh as unobtrusively as possible and only enough to allow the marsh to teach you its secrets.

Observations of a Salt Marsh. Visit a salt marsh on a calm summer day and find a spot that will give you an overview of the marsh. Let yourself become aware of this special habitat. Close your eyes and give your other senses a chance. You will hear the sigh of the wind in the grasses, the whine of a mosquito, the burble of a marsh wren, the raucous call of red-winged blackbirds. Listen for the rhythmic, rasping hum of crickets and the annoying buzz of greenhead flies. Feel the warmth of the sun on your knees or the tickle of tiny spider "toes" on your foot. What do you smell? Is it mud or grass? Is the tide high or low? Is it coming in or is it going out? Can you hear the moving water? Do the smells change as the tide comes and goes? Do birds and insects react to the changing water level? Can you hear the clicks and snaps of marine animals like hermit crabs?

After several minutes, make a list of the bits of information about this habitat that you've collected through your various senses. If your notes seem more like poetry than nature study, don't be surprised.

A Look at the Spartinas (Primarily on the east coast). From the spot where you can see the whole marsh, you can observe not only the subtle color, texture, and height variations between the zones of plant growth, but also where the different species grow relative to each other. If the tidal waters are returning, you'll see water on its landward journey swirl first across the mud flats, then around the roots of *Spartina alterniflora*. If you continue to watch, you will see the tidal water course up into the many creekbeds that wind their way inland. Where does *Spartina alterniflora* grow? Does it grow only at the seaward edge of the marsh or does it also flourish along the edge of marsh creeks? Do the mud flats have any hummocks or isolated mounds of marsh soil that support plant life? Do your observations suggest what plants are growing on them? Does the location of these hummocks suggest that the marsh is spreading out into the mud flats?

Creeks in the Marsh. Are there many creeks meandering through the

rhizomes

roots

Saltwater cordgrass
(Spartina alterniflora)

marsh? Do any of the creeks seem to have a freshwater origin at the landward side of the marsh? Do you see any drainage ditches? These are man-made and can be distinguished from natural marsh creeks by their straight path through the marsh. These ditches were dug as a mosquito control tactic. Do you observe any pools of water within the marsh where mosquitoes might breed?

On a Stormy Day. On a windy day when the tide is in and the waves are high, visit the salt marsh. Observe the action of the water as it surges into the cordgrass, *Spartina alterniflora* (*Spartina foliosa* on the west coast). Can you see how this grass affects the waves and turbulence of the water? Does this suggest the value of *Spartina alterniflora* to the developing marsh? If this marsh falls prey to the developers, what will substitute for the alterniflora's contribution to the stability of the shoreline?

In Late Summer or Early Fall. Look for an expanse of *Spartina patens* in the higher, open area of the marsh. It is distinguished by a swirling pattern where the grasses are lying flat on the marsh. This pattern is called "cowlicks," because of its resemblance to the unruly hair of a child. Later in the fall, the golden hues of the seeding grasses give the scene a special beauty. This salt hay was once harvested in the fall by farmers for cattle feed. Snip a spartina close to the soil. Examine the stem carefully. Can you see the narrow area where the stem folds over?

A Comparison of the Spartinas. Where is *Spartina patens* growing relative to *Spartina alterniflora*? Are both grasses the same shade of green? If not, how are they different? Get closer to the spartinas. Are both species of spartina the same height? What is an average difference? Are the leaf blades of both species the same size? How much bigger or smaller, wider or longer is the blade of one species than that of the other? What other differences can you see? Make a list of them. Are there similarities between the two grasses? Record them. (See Chapter Note 1 for some of these comparisons.)

A Close-up of Cordgrass Roots. One good place to observe the root system of *Spartina alterniflora* is from a marsh creek while sitting in a rowboat at mid-tide or low tide. Pull on a grass plant without actually trying to remove it and without damaging it. Do you think that it would be easy to remove? What is the advantage of this to the plant and to a developing marsh? Often the root systems of *Spartina alterniflora* are exposed along the creek banks. What

Saltmeadow grass (Spartina patens)

do the roots look like? Is there a single long taproot or are the roots growing in a branching pattern? How do you think this pattern of root development helps the plant? How is this root growth pattern helpful to the marsh as a whole? What other life forms do you observe among the tangle of roots? Look for the holes made by fiddler crabs. Record your observations in your notebook.

Reproduction in the Spartinas. Spartina and other grasses reproduce in two ways. The most usual method is asexual: the plant sends out underground stems, or rhizomes, from which new plants develop. The spartinas also reproduce sexually by producing seeds, which develop from the union of male and female sex cells. Go to a marsh in early summer and use your hand lens to view the tiny flowers that have developed on the spikes on the very top of the spartina stems. These grass flowers are pollinated by the wind. What other plants can you think of that have inconspicuous flowers and are pollinated by the wind? Return to the marsh in late summer. This time, look for the tiny seeds that have developed on the flower spikes. The seeds give it a fuzzy appearance. A hand lens will improve your view.

EXPLORATIONS

The following activities require that you closely observe other plants that make the marsh their home. Since you will probably need to touch the plants, do so only if you can find them growing beside established pathways in the marsh.

Grasses. Although most of the dominant plants growing in the marsh resemble grasses, three distinct botanical families are represented. They are the grasses, the sedges, and the rushes. As you have already discovered, the spartinas are true grasses, because they have hollow, generally round stems with solid bumps, called joints, where the leaves are attached. Another characteristic of grasses is that the veins of the narrow grass leaves run parallel to each other.

You will find the following grasses, sedges, and rushes at the landward edge of the *Spartina patens* territory. These plants grow among the patens grasses. Look among the patens for something different. Then use the following guide to see which of the other common marsh plants you have found.

Spike Grass (Distichlis spicata), Found on the East and West Coasts: Look for the leaf veins that run parallel to each other. You will also notice that the base of the leaf is wrapped around the stem, while the remainder of the leaf is not. This sheath, often compared to a tube slit down on one side, is a characteristic of grasses. Sometimes it's very difficult to distinguish spike grass from *Spartina patens* during the growing season. There are some clues that will help you separate spike grass from its look-alike, *Spartina patens*. First, spike grass has

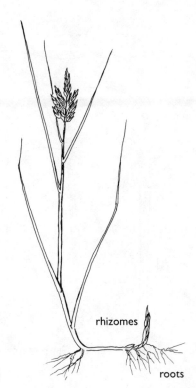

rhizomes

roots

Spike grass (Distichlis spicata)

light green leaves. The leaves of patens are a darker shade of green. Second, look for stiff stems. The eight- to fifteen-inch stems of spike grass are very stiff compared with the stems of patens. Also, the dead, curly, tan leaves of last year's growth of spike grass persist close to this year's new growth. Another clue is the sandy soil that spike grass prefers over the muddy soil that *Spartina patens* prefers. With the aid of your hand lens, make a drawing of spike grass. Don't forget to use colors.

Sedges, Found on the East and West Coasts: In addition to the grasses, the salt marsh is home to sedges. Unlike grass stems, "the stems of sedges have edges." Also, unlike the hollow stems of grasses, the stems of sedges are solid. If you make a horizontal cut through the stem of a sedge, you can see the triangular shape of the stem, which is characteristic of these marsh perennials. You can feel this triangular shape when you roll the stem between your thumb and forefinger. The rhizomes of sedges are food for muskrats and geese, while the seeds are eaten by ducks and other marsh birds. Make a drawing of your sedge and be sure to indicate the differences between it and spike grass.

Rushes, Found on the East and West Coasts: The zone of the black rush, *Juncus gerardi*, is the highest level of the marsh that saltwater reaches when

Sedge or saltmarsh bulrush (Scirpus robustus)

Black grass (Juncus gerardi)

storm surges and spring tides coincide. This plant is often inappropriately called black grass. It is not a grass. Look for *Juncus* in late spring when it is dark green and grass-like. The stem is round, but unlike grasses, there is no node present. If you look for black grass in the fall, you will see its dark, almost black seeds, which give the plant its common name and make it easy to identify. Another helpful clue is that it grows in dense clumps. Make a drawing of black grass. In March or April, a hand lens will help you to observe the tiny flowers on this rush.

The Salicornias, Found on the East and West Coasts: As you searched the upper marsh for the sedges and rushes, you probably encountered one of the most interesting of marsh plants, the mysterious glasswort. From Nova Scotia to Georgia, glassworts of one species or another grow in almost all of our salt marshes. You can look for the perennial *Salicornia virginica* (woody glasswort) and the annual *Salicornia europaea* in salt pans or shallow depressions, since they prefer living where the salinity of the soil is very high. *Salicornia europaea* is especially easy to find in the fall, since it turns a beautiful red-orange, adding a splash of color to the autumn marsh. The early settlers to New England called this plant "pickle-wort" and used it to add flavor to salads.

These six- to fifteen-inch plants, fleshy, cactus-like, and smooth, are easy

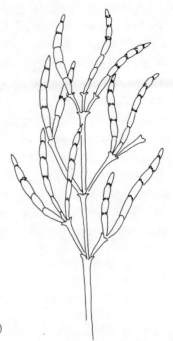

Jointed glasswort (Salicornia europaea)

to find. Does the salicornia branch like a small tree as it grows or does it grow in a bunch of single, nonbranching stalks? With the aid of a hand lens, look for the tiny leaves that lie flat against the succulent stems. Sometimes you can find a salicornia that's been uprooted. What kind of root system does it have? What advantage does a succulent have in this environment? Collect as much information as you can from your observations and write a description of the plants. What other plants are growing in the immediate vicinity? With the aid of your hand lens, make a drawing of the salicornia and add it to your permanent field notebook.

A Profile of Your Marsh. Using the illustration below as a guide, draw a profile of your marsh. Indicate the landward border of the marsh, as well as the line of mean low water and the line of mean high water. Don't forget to mark off the region touched by the spring tides. On the profile, show the places in the marsh where specific plants grow and their positions relative to other marsh plants and tidal waters.

CHAPTER NOTES

1. **A Comparison of the Spartinas.** *Spartina alterniflora* and *Spartina patens* differ a great deal in appearance. *Spartina alterniflora* is much larger and grows to a height of six to ten feet along marsh creeks and ditches, although it

is generally shorter as it grows inland along the creeks and away from the water's edge. At their bases, the leaves of *Spartina alterniflora* may be twice as wide as those of *Spartina patens*. Salt marsh cordgrass grows in fairly dense stands where little light penetrates to the mud below, creating a warm, humid environment in which many organisms, including decomposers, thrive. In contrast, *Spartina patens* is a finer grass and has a more delicate appearance. It produces a very dense meadow of grass, which effectively keeps other plants from competing with it. Its location in the marsh permits twice-monthly drenching by the spring tides. This is necessary for the grass to reproduce.

Since it spends most of its time out of the salt water, *Spartina patens* does not use quite so much of its energy to maintain salt balance. Thus, you can see that plant zonation in the marsh is related to the degree of exposure and inundation during the tidal cycle.

CHAPTER 12

The Mud Snail

A TINY CARNIVORE

Of the many natural intertidal communities, mud flats, unlike tide pools and salt marshes, are generally considered unattractive, inhospitable, and barren wastelands. For most people, mud flats are simply smelly, mushy places where walking is difficult and insects flourish, places that are, at best, ignored. Consequently, most beachcombers are unaware that this habitat is extremely fertile and teeming with life.

Mud flat intertidal regions are formed at the mouth of an estuary or at the edge of a salt marsh. They also develop along the bottom of shallow embayments. The type of mud and the quality of the bottom is determined by the kinds of sediments that are carried by the water and deposited. For example, flats made of a mix of water and tiny particles of silt and clay will be extremely yielding. The flats are difficult to walk across without sinking into the thick, brown mud up to your ankles or even up to your hips. In contrast, mud flats of water and larger sand grains are firm and easily explored. Additionally, since intertidal animals are sensitive to the size of sediment particles, different communities or organisms will be found on each type of mud flat.

The receding tide often lays temporary carpets of algae, such as bright green sheets of sea lettuce (*Ulva*) and deep green threads of gut weed (*Enteromorpha*) on the surface of the mud. Microscopic life forms, which are more permanent residents on the mud flats, cast a lavender hue over the somber gray-brown mud. These tiny plants and animals, spread lavishly over the mud surface by the tidal steward, contribute to the productivity of the mud flats. These habitats are able to support a variety of animals with a diversity of feeding adaptations. Shore birds with long beaks gather, clamor, and probe the mud for edibles. Among them, dowitchers feed like sewing machines, while knots in tightly knit flocks share the bounty with black-bellied plovers, all feasting on tiny crustaceans, mollusks, marine worms, and insects. In response to tidal signals, polychaete worms that live below the mud surface send up elaborately fringed tentacles, which collect another meal of plankton. Thus, nearly everywhere you look on a mud flat, there is life and growth.

Perhaps the animal most closely associated with a mud flat community, especially near the low-tide line, is the eastern mud snail. (See Chapter Note 1 for the snail's west coast range.) Its technical name, *Illyanassa obsoletus*, comes from both Latin and Greek. The first name, *illy* (Greek) plus *nassa* (Latin), means "muddy fishing basket," while its second name is from the Latin word meaning "worn out" or "obsolete." A careful look at the mud snail's dingy, olive-brown shell, often encrusted with mud and algae, reveals the appropriateness of its name, while the dilapidated appearance gives a clue to the grueling conditions of life in the intertidal zone. The vast numbers of mud snails found at low tide, frequently as many as a thousand per square meter, is a testimony to their biological success and places them among the major inhabitants of mud flats and other estuarine communities.

Illyanassa belongs to the large group of animals called mollusks. Within the phylum, they are members of the class that is formally named Gastropod, which literally means "stomach-foot." Like all snails, *Illyanassa* is a univalve (one-shelled) and feeds with its file-like tongue called a radula.

The snails are often mistaken for small black stones cast on the mud surface, but a patient observer will see the throngs of "pebbles" come to life as they glide along the thin film of water left on the mud by the retreating sea. This gliding activity leaves a web of characteristic trails on the mud surface. Mud snails are nimble, possessing an agility not generally seen in snails. You can easily experience this by putting a mud snail in your hand with the open side of the shell facing up. Watch as the supple snail body begins to twist and turn as the snail tries to turn itself upright. This skill is beneficial to an animal that is often tossed about by churning tidal waters.

Illyanassa are deposit feeders, which means that they feed on microscopic plant plankton. Their diet is especially rich in those phytoplankton called diatoms. These tiny plants, often referred to by microscope users as "the jewels of the sea," are the most abundant plants living in cold waters. Like all plants, they are able to capture the sun's energy; then, using inorganic substances like nitrogen, carbon dioxide, and water, diatoms transform the solar energy into living plant material. These tiny plants, or "producers," are the foundation of the marine ecosystem.

Because mud snails feed on plant material, they are called herbivores. They graze by using their radulae to gather diatoms and other microscopic plants

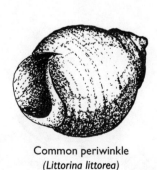

Common periwinkle
(*Littorina littorea*)

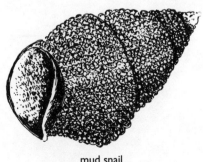

mud snail
(*Illyanassa obsoletus*)

Two often-confused intertidal snails

THE MUD SNAIL

that cover the soft mud. Grazers such as these feed near the base of the food chain, and through metabolic processes, they convert living plant material into living snail tissue and energy. For this reason they are called primary consumers.

Another ecological niche that mud snails fill is that of scavenger. As part of nature's clean-up crew, they consume dead clams, fishes, and other carrion. This second feeding ability of mud snails makes them also part of the group of secondary consumers. They are adapted to this latter role by having extremely long and flexible siphons, or tubes, that can be extended. With the aid of specialized cells within the siphon, mud snails can detect minute amounts of chemicals in the water from dead and decaying material. Guided by the chemical "smell," armies of *Illyanassa* close in on the next meal. However, if the scent is that of dead mud snails, the army makes a hasty retreat!

Life for mud snails is not always as tranquil as it might seem. They are preyed upon by a variety of waterfowl, like black ducks, and fishes, such as cod and haddock. These predators, through a series of chemical steps, convert snail tissue into bird and fish protein. Thus, the organic molecules, manufactured by the diatoms from raw materials and the sun's energy, travel in a series of steps from one organism to another. It is along these steps, or links, that food chains move life-supporting nutrients and energy. Unfortunately, pollutants and toxic materials also travel along these pathways and thus are able to reach other members of the earth community.

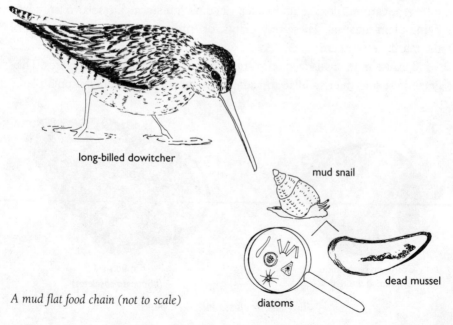

long-billed dowitcher

mud snail

dead mussel

A mud flat food chain (not to scale)

diatoms

THE WORLD OF THE MUD SNAIL

What you will need	Science skills
basic kit	observing
thermometer	collecting data
toothpicks or pieces of straw	measuring
two wire coat hangers	comparing
waterproof marker	
watch with a second hand	
soupspoon or trowel	
tape measure	
patience	

OBSERVATIONS

Spring and Summer Observations

Mud Snail Trails. I have found that some of the most accessible mud flats are located where roads cross salt marsh areas. Along the edges of these roads and at the bridges over the tidal creeks, you can get a close view of mud flats and even reach into the mud without becoming too muddy yourself. Search the flats for a population of mud snails at low tide. Observe the trails made by mud snails as they glide along on the thin film of water left by the receding tide. What sort of path do the snails take? Do they move in a straight line or is the path curved? Do the snails cross each other's paths as they glide across the mud? Is there a pattern to their paths (for instance, toward the water) or are their motions random? Do you observe any abrupt changes in direction? Do they seem to favor a right or a left turn? Do path lengths vary much from one snail to another? Does air temperature seem to influence how long the trails are? (Observe the snail trails on both warm and cool days.) Do the snails move and pause frequently? Can you infer where they seem to be going? Is there evidence that they are territorial? Can you conclude whether they are solitary or social animals? What evidence do you have for your conclusions?

Other Members of the Mud Flat Community. You have been observing a population (a group of individuals of the same species) of mud snails that lies within specific boundaries. The mud snail population is part of a larger community, which is made up of other living things. Make a list of other creatures that you find in the community. You will want to indicate whether the other animals are permanent residents, like various clam species, or transients, such as herring gulls.

THE MUD SNAIL 135

EXPLORATIONS
Spring and Summer Explorations

Measuring the Speed of a Snail's Pace. Build a little flag with a toothpick or a bit of straw. Place this "flag" next to a mud snail moving in its natural habitat, or use a natural marker in the mud. Now measure, or estimate, how far the snail goes in five minutes. Repeat this several times and average your results. Based on this figure, calculate how many centimeters per hour constitutes a "snail's pace." Can you calculate a snail's pace in miles per hour?

Observations of a Single Snail. Try to capture a single mud snail without joining the mud flat community yourself. A long, flat stick might help in this task. Put your mud snail on a glass pie plate or a piece of clear, colorless plastic. Looking from below this platform, observe the rhythmic contractions of the snail's foot. Does the mud snail leave a mucous trail on the glass? How might that help the snail's forward movement?

Reaction to Touch. With the aid of your hand lens, find the tentacles, eyes, and siphon of the mud snail. Gently touch the snail's head with an object such as a tiny piece of straw. What did the snail do? Touch it with your finger. Does it react in the same way or differently? How does the mud snail react when it bumps into an object like a stone or a small stick?

Observing Groups of Snails. The next step is to observe a group of mud snails. This is a logical step because mud snails frequently feed in groups. To investigate this behavior, gather about six mud snails, put them on a clean pie plate, and observe them moving around the plate for five minutes or so. Do they tend to stay isolated or do they tend to form one or more groups? Make a sketch as a record of what they do. Carefully remove them.

Next place one new snail on the plate. Observe the movements of this snail on the plate. Does it move randomly or does it move in the same direction as

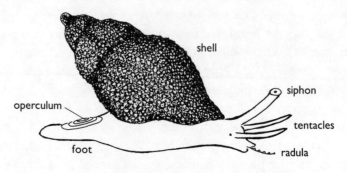

Mud snail (Illyanassa obsoletus)

the original group did? Does this mud snail seem to follow the trails left by the other mud snails? What you are observing is a mud snail's response to chemicals left by members of its own species. What advantage is this chemoreception for mud snails? (See Chapter Note 2 for some information on chemical trails.)

Investigating Other Aspects of Chemoreception. Mud snails fill two ecological niches. They are scavengers and carnivores. Since the flats often are covered with mud snails, many get crushed accidentally by beach strollers. Find one of these freshly killed snails, and after it has been dead for several hours, place it on the surface of the mud in the vicinity of a group of mud snails. How do the snails react? Try this with a piece of chopped meat or chicken that has begun to "go bad." How do the snails react? What are the implications of this behavior for the survival of the mud snail population? Did individual mud snails respond in a similar way or differently to the dead group member? (This exploration could also be carried out on the pie plate.)

Estimating Populations of Mud Snails. You have probably noticed that there are hordes of mud snails roaming the tidal flats. To count all of the individuals in the mud snail population would take a very long time. However, with a method called sampling, you can estimate the size of the population. Make a one-foot square with the wire from old coat hangers or any other material that will give you a rigid frame. This device is called a quadrat. Quadrats can be larger if you are studying a very big area.

Walk out onto the mud flat (make sure that the mud flat you choose for this exploration is of the firm variety!) and gently toss your square, letting it fall where it will. Count the number of mud snails within the square. Try the hanger toss several more times. Keep a record of the number of snails counted in each toss by making a chart similar to the one below.

NUMBER OF SNAILS
IN EACH QUADRAT SAMPLE

Trial #	Snail Count
1	_____
2	_____
3	_____
Total	_____

The next step is to estimate the size of the mud flat by pacing it and multiplying the length by the width. Your sampling technique provides an average number of snails per square foot. Multiply this number by the area of the mud flat to provide an estimate of the number of mud snails on the mud flat.

TOTAL NUMBER OF SNAILS
ON THE MUD FLAT

$$\text{length of flat} \times \text{width of flat} \times \text{average number of snails per square foot} = \text{total}$$

$$\underline{\hspace{2cm}} \times \underline{\hspace{2cm}} \times \underline{\hspace{2cm}} = \underline{\hspace{2cm}}$$

There are 40,000 square feet in an acre. How many mud snails would there be in an acre of mud flat according to your results?

$$40,000 \times \text{average number of snails per square foot} = \text{number per acre}$$

$$40,000 \times \underline{\hspace{2cm}} = \underline{\hspace{2cm}}$$

Fall and Winter Explorations

Vertical Migration. Mud snails don't go to Florida for the winter. Instead, they burrow deep below the surface of the mud during the cold months. You can find out what a good strategy this is if you take the temperature of the mud at different depths. Begin this exploration on a very cold day. Measure the temperature on the surface of the mud. Use a trowel or an old soupspoon to dig holes in the mud four, eight, and twelve inches below the surface. (Watch out for buried animals.) What did you discover about the temperature as you went deeper? How does this explain the advantages of vertical migration for mud snails with the onset of cold weather?

How Deep Mud Snails Burrow. On a brisk autumn day before the extremely cold weather of winter, you can find out something about the distance mud snails will migrate. Dig into the mud, but while doing so, be careful not to hurt the animals. You'll be surprised at how deep the snails burrow even before it gets very cold.

Visit the same mud flat on a warm day in midwinter. You may find that some of the snails have left their burrows for a few hours of feeding.

Food Chains. By observing what mud snails eat and what eats mud snails, you can now construct a food chain. Can you construct more than one food chain involving the mud snail? (See Chapter Note 3 for some possible food chain hints.)

CHAPTER NOTES

1. **The Mud Snail on the West Coast.** The eastern mud snail (*Illyanassa obsoletus*) has an extensive range on the west coast. It thrives on the mud flats from Vancouver Island, British Columbia, to central California.

2. **Chemical Traces.** Many marine organisms leave chemical traces, which are detected by members of their species. The chemical trails are helpful to the individuals and to the group when it comes to essential activities, such as finding food, avoiding predators, and keeping the group together.

3. **Food Chains.**
   a. dead fish > mud snail > black duck
   b. diatoms > mud snail > cod fish > man

CHAPTER 13

Shore Birds

HUNGRY VISITORS

The infant light of the new day creeps imperceptibly above the horizon. Its pale orange hue washes across the skyline and gives a flickering sheen to the still sleeping sea. The air of the early spring morning is filled with the raucous screams of gulls as they scribe circles in the gray-blue sky. Life on the sandy mud flats is awakening. One by one, small birds come to feed. Then, seeming to materialize out of nowhere, hundreds of shore birds can be seen darting over the expanse of the muddy plain. The arrival of migrating beach birds is an awesome sight.

Running, darting, pecking, and probing, each bird a metabolic marvel, they seek fuel for the hungry fires that burn within their tiny, feathered bodies. Eating is nonstop. The frenetic activity calls into question the old saw about "eating like a bird."

The smallest of the warm-blooded animals to make a living from the intertidal zone, shore birds take advantage of the enormous number of beach fleas, worms, mollusks, crabs, and other invertebrates that make their homes on and under the sand and mud flats. It's been estimated that as many as thirty-five hundred of these invertebrates live in every square meter of a sandbar, while the same area of the more organic mud flats supports over eight thousand of these energy-rich tidbits.

This intertidal cornucopia is especially important to the birds, because the metabolic rate of a bird (the rate at which the birds use energy) is very high.

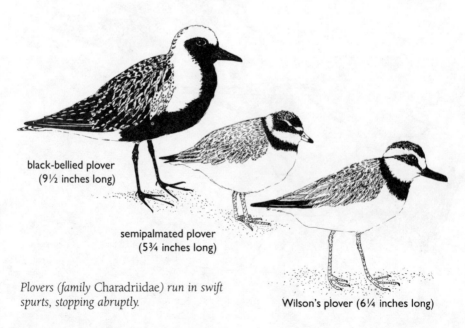

black-bellied plover
(9½ inches long)

semipalmated plover
(5¾ inches long)

Plovers (family Charadriidae*) run in swift spurts, stopping abruptly.*

Wilson's plover (6¼ inches long)

This is because flying is an energy-intensive activity and because birds must maintain a constant internal temperature of 101 degrees Fahrenheit. Animals with such high metabolism rates need to eat high-energy foods, such as insects and fish, which are rich in proteins and fats.

It has been estimated that plovers, fairly large beach birds that weigh about 190 grams, eat 33 percent of their body weight per day. Small, 30-gram, sparrow-sized sandpipers will eat about 55 percent of their body weight in the same time period. Putting this information into more familiar terms, a 180-pound man would have to eat 100 pounds of meat each day to approximate the nutrient requirements of these little birds. Fortunately, larger animals have lower metabolic rates. The smaller the bird, the larger the amount of food it must eat, relative to body weight.

Although the amount of food eaten by the birds is substantial, it not only must satisfy their minimum daily requirements, but it also must include those additional calories needed to defend their territories, feed their young, or gain the weight vital to successful long-distance flights into the Canadian marshes and Arctic tundra. Beach birds have developed some fabulous tools and behaviors for finding and harvesting the tiny creatures so essential to their survival.

One of the bird families that visits these migratory truck stops is the plovers. Plovers use the "run-and-stab" approach to food getting. The heavy bill of the Wilson plover is ideal for stabbing crabs, while the slender bill of the semipalmated plover is more suited for spearing softer prey, such as polychaete worms and brachiopods. The black-bellied plover, the largest member of this family, uses the same stabbing technique as the smaller family members, but it is faster afoot, runs longer distances, and catches larger prey.

Another group of beach birds is the sandpipers. This large group of birds is noted for its physical diversity in body type, neck length, and bill size and shape. Sandpipers also show diversity in behaviors such as habitat preference and foraging technique. Many of them are peckers and probers; others are waders. Each species of bird makes its living from its own technique and has its own characteristic bill especially designed for its task. The bills are equipped with special sensory organs that allow the bird to feel its way beneath the mud. Scientists have found that the sensory receptors localized in the tips of sandpiper bills can detect vibrations made by worms and other prey that live in the sand. The flexible tips also facilitate grasping and removal of prey.

The least sandpiper is a fast paced pecker, feeding on invertebrates that live on the mud and sand. It doesn't probe for the deeper-dwelling snails and shrimps like its cousin, the semipalmated sandpiper, does (or the western

least sandpiper (4¾ inches long)

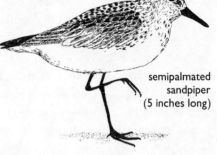

semipalmated sandpiper (5 inches long)

The least sandpiper has greenish-yellow legs and is browner than other small sandpipers.

Often confused with the least sandpiper, the semipalmated sandpiper is lighter in color and has black legs and bill.

sandpiper on the west coast). On the other hand, sanderlings often run along the beach in large groups, pecking mole crabs from retreating waves, while a relative, the purple sandpiper (or the rock sandpiper on the west coast), picks rock crevices for nourishment left by the falling tide. Short-billed dowitchers prefer to feed in silent flocks and can be seen along the flats with their heads often underwater as they probe the bottom with rapid stitching movements.

In addition to the techniques perfected by these beach birds, a separate group of sandpipers makes its living strolling in the shallows or along the edge of the swash zone. The yellowlegs, godwits, willets, and curlews are among these waders.

Yellowlegs, unlike some of their gregarious relatives, are solitary birds. They slowly wade in the shallows and sweep the water's surface with their long bills, capturing the larger and more mobile prey, such as minnows and other

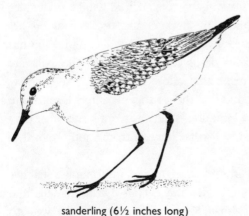

sanderling (6½ inches long)

The sanderling is reddish in spring and white and gray with black markings in fall and winter.

short-billed dowitcher (9½ inches long)

The dowitcher has a white wedge on its rump and a barred tail.

small fish. This behavior contrasts with the long-legged willets, which run down the sandy flats in pursuit of crabs and other edibles that have been spilled onto the beach by breaking waves. The uptilted bill of the godwits equips this bird for vigorous probing after large, deeply buried prey, such as lugworms and razor clams. The down-curved bill of curlews makes these birds experts in probing burrows and removing the most stubborn prey.

American oystercatchers (or the black American oystercatcher on the west coast) and another specialized sandpiper, the ruddy turnstone (the black turnstone on the west coast), are equipped with sturdy, flat bills for chiseling and hammering food. With great skill, oystercatchers make surprise attacks on relaxing mollusks with slightly open shells. The precise thrust of the bill severs the adductor muscles that hold the mollusk shell closed. Once this muscle is cut, it's "mussels on the half shell" for the hungry oystercatcher. Often taking

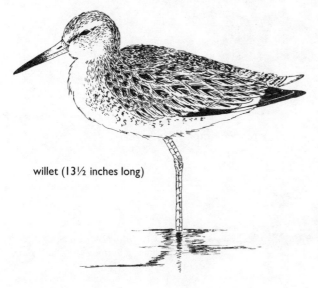

willet (13½ inches long)

This large shorebird is best identified by the bold black-and-white pattern on its wings and rather long blue-gray legs.

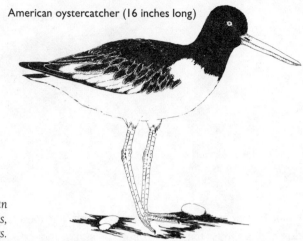

American oystercatcher (16 inches long)

This spectacular bird has an orange-red bill, yellow eyes, and thick pink legs.

as long as a year to perfect this technique, young oystercatchers must be satisfied with morsels parceled out by their parents until the young can master shell opening.

Turnstones also have a unique hunting procedure. As their name implies, they are often seen flipping over shells and stones as they search for their meals, and since four eyes are often more efficient than two, the birds frequently work in pairs. These birds are also skilled at digging holes, often bigger than themselves, in which they find tiny crustaceans and mollusks.

ruddy turnstone (7 inches long)

This chunky bird has a slender, slightly upturned bill and short orange-red legs.

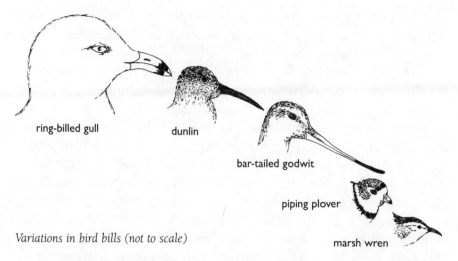

ring-billed gull

dunlin

bar-tailed godwit

piping plover

marsh wren

Variations in bird bills (not to scale)

Each species of shore bird has developed different techniques for getting its food. This diversity reduces direct competition between them. However, despite the specializations in behavior, in bill length and shape, and so on, most birds will not go hungry if the ideal type of food is not available. Scientists find that birds eat what they can get rather than being specialists. Research into the preferred diets of beach bird species indicates that the birds eat such a variety of marine organisms that it is impossible to draw one single meaningful food web from the tangle of possible food chains that are found on the beach and mud flat. This ability of birds to adapt quickly to available food supplies is one key to their success.

THE WORLD OF SHORE BIRDS

What you will need
- basic kit
- compass
- binoculars
- field guide to birds
- tape measure
- tenacity

Science skills
- observing
- recording
- inferring
- grouping
- gathering data
- measuring

OBSERVATIONS

At first glance, all of the little birds that flock to the sand and mud flats to feed look distressingly alike. However, if you spend some time watching them, you will slowly begin to notice several distinct body types and behavioral patterns. As you pay close attention to these, the job of deciding who's who in the world of these birds will become much less confusing. You'll find that a field guide will be easier to use if you first learn to observe the birds' general features and then to make behavioral observations.

Grouping Shore Birds. Select an intertidal habitat, such as a mud flat or salt marsh, and make yourself comfortable without being intrusive. For a few minutes, observe the many different kinds of birds that come to the area. Since so many different birds visit the sandy beach and the mud flats, you will often see a dozen or more birds scurrying helter-skelter in what seems to be a maze of confusion. At first, don't try to observe every detail; just see if you can divide the birds into two or three different groups of similar birds. What cues did you use to put the birds into the different groups? Usually, the first thing you tend to notice is size—big birds and little birds. Then if you persist, you will notice other differences: bills, necks, legs, tails, shape, and markings, like neck or beak rings. As you keep looking, you'll notice a variety of distinctive behaviors, such as walking versus running and unusual feeding motions.

Observing Bird Anatomy. Select a bird from one of the groups that particularly interests you. Look at its general size and shape. Is your bird about the size of a sparrow? If so, its body is about six inches long. Or is your bird more like a robin, with a body about ten inches long? Perhaps its size approximates that of a crow, about twenty inches long. Is the bird plump, thin, stubby, or streamlined?

Bill Types: Observe the bill. Is it long, short, thick, or thin? Is the bill straight or curved? Does it curve up or down? What color is it? Use the bill of a

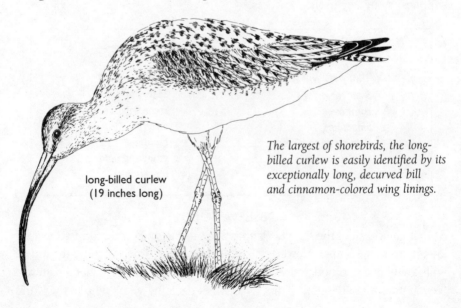

long-billed curlew
(19 inches long)

The largest of shorebirds, the long-billed curlew is easily identified by its exceptionally long, decurved bill and cinnamon-colored wing linings.

purple sandpiper
(7½ inches long)

The darkest of the sandpipers, this plump bird has dull yellow or orange at the base of its bill and on its short legs.

bird you already know to make these comparisons. The familiar herring gull is generally a good standard to use.

Tail Variations: Observe the tail. Is it long? (Compare it with the tails of suggested birds in your bird field guide.) Two birds with relatively long tails are the cuckoo and the brown thrasher. Is the tail of medium length like that of a cardinal or short like that of a starling? Is the tail forked like a swallow's or rounded like a blue jay's? Is it pointed or square-tipped? Does it have a white stripe or white edges?

Proportions: Look for proportions. How long are the legs relative to the body length? How long is the bill relative to the head? Is the neck long or short?

yellowlegs

A tall, long-legged sandpiper, the greater yellowlegs (11 inches long) is distinguished from the lesser yellowlegs (8¾ inches long) by its greater overall size and longer bill.

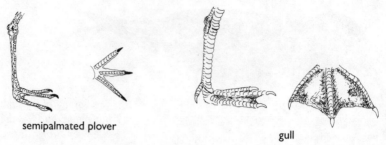

semipalmated plover

gull

Variations in bird feet

Legs: Are the legs long or short? What color are the legs and feet? Are the feet webbed? Are the toes long?

Wings: Are the wings pointed or rounded? When the wings are folded, what is their position relative to the tip of the tail? Do the wings extend beyond the tail?

The following chart might be helpful in organizing your information.

Since writing helps us clarify concepts, write a description of the bird based on your observations. The next time you're at the beach, see if you can find the same type of bird, using your notes as a guide. If not, what important information did you leave out?

Observing Bird Behavior. Now focus on the bird's behavior. What is its flight pattern? Does it glide, flap, soar? Are the wing beats fast, slow, or stiff? Is the flight path straight or is it undulating like a roller coaster? How does the bird use its tail when it lands?

Describe the bird's gait. Does it run, hop, walk, or stalk? How does it hold its body when it moves?

DISTINCTIVE CHARACTERISTICS OF BIRDS

	Bird #1	Bird #2	Bird #3
Size			
Shape			
Beak			
Colors and patterns			
Legs and feet			
Wings			
Other features			

Describe the bird's eating behavior. Does it stab the sand or mud? Does it use its beak like the needle of a sewing machine or like a chisel?

Social Behavior. Is your bird a solitary bird or is it part of a flock? Is the group large (greater than ten birds) or is it small (less than ten birds)?

The Field Guide. Once you have made detailed observations of the physical characteristics and the behaviors of several different kinds of shore birds, you will find it easy to use a field guide to the birds. In some cases, you may find that several small birds in the book look much like one of your birds. This is where your location may be important. Check the range of the birds; very often only one of the possible birds will be at your location at a particular time of the year.

EXPLORATIONS

Bird Tracks. Bird tracks make an interesting study. Among the best places to find them are on sandy beaches near the water's edge or on mud flats at low tide. Select an area. How many sets of tracks can you find? How many different kinds of birds made the tracks? Which type of tracks are the most frequent? Select a series of tracks that you think were made by one bird. How far apart are the tracks? What do you think the bird was doing? Hopping? Walking? Running?

Look for evidence of a bird's pecking and probing in the sand. Where do you find the most evidence of feeding? Close to the swash line, near the strand line, or other places?

Make a map to show the path a bird traveled across the mud or sand. Select another set of tracks. Using a different color, make another path map. What do these maps tell you? Use a compass to determine the primary direction in which the birds traveled. How far did each bird move in that direction? In what other directions did they travel and for what distance? What was the greatest distance each bird traveled from the time it landed on the sand until its tracks were no longer discernible?

Observe a variety of birds as they walk in the sand or mud. When they fly off, observe and draw their distinctive tracks. With the combined help of your field guide and your own observations, find out the names of these birds. If you develop the ability to identify a bird solely from its tracks, you are on your way to becoming a beach bird expert!

Habitat Observations. Go to a few different coastal habitats, such as the salt marsh, rocky shore, or a dune system. Do the same kinds of birds visit each of these different habitats? Are there different kinds of birds in each of these habitats? Do you find that some types of birds are "generalists" and are

BIRDS AND THEIR SHORE HABITATS

Habitat	Specialists	Generalists
Salt marsh		
Rocky shore		
Tidal flats		
Sandy beach		
Sand dunes		

found in all of the habitats? Do you find that some bird types are specialists and are found in only one type of habitat? Use the chart above to organize your findings.

Are the birds seasonal visitors or do they visit the habitats throughout the year? If you only see them during the summer, when do they visit? In June, July, August, and/or September? Which habitat seems to have the most variety of birds? Can you explain why this is so?

Visit these habitats during the winter months. Make a list of the different kinds of birds you see. What do they eat?

A look at herons

little blue heron

little green heron

snowy egret

great blue heron

(not to scale)

Observing Herons. Members of taxonomic or scientific groups generally bear resemblance to one another. Consider the herons. They illustrate the concept very well, and the salt marsh is a good place to find members of this group. Find a few different species in your area and order them according to size.

The largest of the wading herons, the great blue heron, can wade in water that's about eighteen inches deep without getting its feathers wet. Using this measure as a standard, what would you say is the maximum wading depth for the following herons: snowy egret (east and Gulf coasts), little blue (east and Gulf coasts), green-backed, tricolored (east and Gulf coasts), great egret, black-crowned night heron, and yellow-crowned night heron?

What are the hunting techniques of each of these herons? Does the heron stab or grab? Estimate the size of the fish that a heron eats. How is the fish swallowed? Whole? Head first? Tail first? Does it matter whether the fish is swallowed head or tail first? Why?

Different species of herons often nest in the same tree. How many species can you find in one tree? Which species has the greatest number of individuals?

CHAPTER 14

Mud Worms

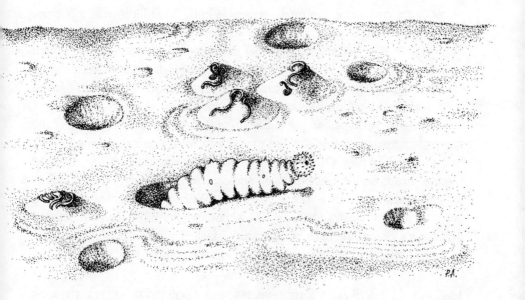

HIDDEN LINKS IN FOOD CHAINS

In these times of international intrigue, large and small wars, and other nefarious happenings, you can be certain that the mud flats of our coastal communities will receive very little media attention. In fact, it's probably safe to say that among the general population, relatively few people are worrying about these mud fields that appear twice daily in the intertidal area as the tide recedes from our estuaries and embayments.

Unknown to most people, the mud flats are teeming with life. In fact, recent research findings tell us that they are the suppliers of the nutrient-rich broth essential to the newly emergent life forms that are developing in the adjacent salt marshes. Often, the thick, brown mud is covered with the opalescent amber of diatoms, which are microscopic algae that colonize and flourish there. Bacteria also thrive in the mud; many species are said to be descended from the anaerobic bacteria, the most primitive life forms, which first emerged when our planet had no oxygen in its atmosphere. The anaerobic bacteria still carry out their life-style without oxygen in the blackness beneath the mud surface. Worms, clams, mussels, and other soft-bodied animals also make their homes in tidal mud flats; they are the dominant members of this community. The richness of life present in a tidal flat can be verified by the numbers of birds that go there to feed.

While worms are not everyone's favorite subject, their link to us is significant. Worms are present in this habitat in enormous numbers, and they are extremely important in the ecology of the mud flat system.

Although there are about five thousand species of worms that make their homes in marine habitats, one of the most common is the polychaete, or bristle worm. Since mid-Cambrian times, some five-hundred million years ago, polychaetes have been etching trails in the sea floor. The fossil record reveals the link between these worms and all other annelids: segmentation and repetition of internal body parts. This fact makes these water-dependent worms close cousins of our diligent friend, the earthworm. The polychaete's name is derived from the bristled, paddle-like appendages on each side of every segment.

There are two types of polychaetes that live on the mud flat. One of the groups is predatory. Some of these predatory worms roam the surface of the flats in search of prey. Other predatory worms burrow through the mud and sand by means of alternate expansion and contraction of body muscles, ingesting mud and water as they seek out their prey. When you are combing the mud flat in search of worms, look on the surface of the mud for cone shaped depressions or for little balls of mud neatly stacked at the edge of a hole.

Polychaete worms of the other group are not hunting predators. They are

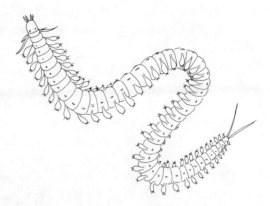

Paddle worm (Eteone trilineata)

sedentary and live more or less permanently inside tube encasements or within burrows below the mud surface. These polychaetes are suspension feeders, which sweep the water column with long and graceful tentacles for a planktonic meal. Some of these tassel-topped worms are equipped with tiny eyes at the end of each tentacle. Others have primitive light receptors that detect only movement. In general, they live a dangerous life, because they have poor vision, slow reflexes, and brightly colored tentacles. Hungry fish wait for the worms to reach up out of their tubes for a meal. When the fish has finished nibbling, the worm must skip a few meals until it grows a new head.

The parchment worm (*Chaetopterus*) is a sedentary polychaete. This worm lives in a long U-shaped tube, which the worm molds from a mixture of sand and its own mucus. You can find this worm at low tide in the very low regions of the intertidal zone. Look for the two ends of the tube, which stick above the surface of the mud. These ends may be far apart, because the parchment worm can build a tube up to two feet long. The worm is creamy yellow and glows in the dark with its own luminescence. It has a distinct head and a variety of appendages along the length of its body. When you see one, you will agree that the parchment worm is a very curious creature.

Like many tube worms, the parchment worm never leaves its tube. It eats by synchronizing the movements of its appendages to create a flow of water into the tube. It then traps plankton in the water using a mucous bag. When the bag is full of plankton, the worm rolls it into a ball about the size of a shotgun pellet and eats it. This is a safer method of eating than waving colorful tentacles out of the tube.

Common wanderers, or errant polychaetes, are the clam worms (sometimes called sandworms in the bait shops), bloodworms, and paddle worms. With specialized structures for a diet of bits of dead fish, small worms, and algae, these worms are rapacious predators. With a polychaete in hand or,

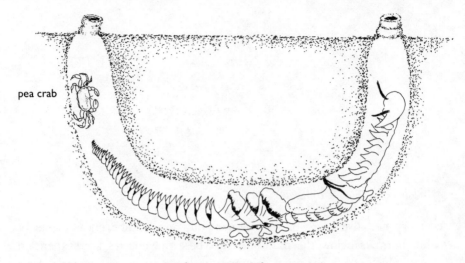

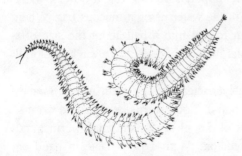

pea crab

Parchment worm (Chaetopterus)

better still, in a plastic container, you might observe a proboscis or protruding mouthpart with its strong jaws that are ideally suited for grasping soft-bodied prey. Held tightly by a pair of powerful teeth, a meal garnished with mud is secured when the proboscis retracts and the food is pulled back into the worm's mouth.

Unlike their less conventional neighbors, polychaete worms are either male or female. During the breeding season, clam worms undergo a curious metamorphosis in which they become special gamete-bearing forms. In this stage of their life, parapodia develop into feathery fins that especially adapt them for swimming. In the darkness of the new moon, with tidal water several feet deep above their mud flat homes, huge masses of polychaete worms swarm to the water's surface and with explosive force release male and female sex cells into the water. With their life purpose completed, the adult clam worms die. They

Blood worm (Glycera dibranchiata)

sink to the bottom to become part of the nitrogen or detritus cycle. Here through the processes of decomposition, the energy locked within their bodies is transformed and used by the thousands of other organisms living in the water.

Meanwhile, the released gametes fuse, and as newly developing larva, the young spend some time as part of the animal plankton drifting here and there with the whims of the current. Not until they are recognizable as clam worms do they join the adult population in the muddy sediment below.

During the daily routine of living, polychaete worms ingest water, sand, and mud containing the nutrient materials that are incorporated into their bodies. Some man-made substances such as PCBs, or polychlorinated biphenyls, may be present in the mud. These pollutants stick to the tiny particles that are taken up by the worms as they feed. Since PCBs do not enter into the ordinary metabolic processes of the worms, they remain incorporated in body tissues. PCBs are not eliminated with digestive waste. The effect is that the deadly PCB chemicals accumulate in the worms, becoming more and more concentrated.

Marine worms are eaten by such delectable human edibles as blue crabs and many of our table fish. This is just one of the mechanisms by which dangerous pollutants get into food chains and food webs and end up in man.

THE WORLD OF MUD WORMS

What you will need	Science skills
basic kit	observing
clear plastic container with lid	recording
dip net	measuring
salad fork	comparing
sieve or screening	
thermometer	
face mask or glass-bottom bucket	
flashlight	
hand lens	
watch with a second hand	
aquarium bubbler and pump	
chipped ice	
small Ziploc bag	
large jar	
waxed paper	
persistence	

OBSERVATIONS

Worms found in the intertidal zone can be grouped in a variety of ways. One method used to classify them is according to their food-getting habits. In this system, errant, or wandering, polychaetes make one group, while sedentary polychaetes form the other. This system is followed in these activities; it is the one used by Kenneth Gosner in the field guide for the Atlantic shore listed in the Bibliography.

You may also find that marine worms are often grouped according to their external appearance: the flatworms, which are flat; the roundworms, which are round; and the segmented worms, whose bodies look like a series of equally spaced rings and which can be either round or flat. Among the most common groups of animals in the tidal flats, the segmented polychaete worms are the marine cousins of our land-bound friends, the earthworms.

Finding the Wandering Polychaetes. You'll find two groups of polychaetes in this habitat. Members of one group, the wanderers, or errant polychaetes, leave their burrows in search of food. Most of these worms are meat eaters with biting jaws appropriate to this life-style, but they won't hurt you if you are careful when collecting them. One of the most common wandering polychaetes is the clam worm, or *Nereis*. These worms roam the tidal flats from the Gulf of St. Lawrence to the tropics. You'll often find them wriggling in tide pools or in intertidal shallows. Their opalescent sheens or rich copper reds and browns make identification relatively simple, especially when you observe the bristles on their many "side feet," or parapodia. The bristled feet give the worms their formal name, since *poly* means "many" and *chaete* means "bristles." Do you find them at any particular time in the tidal cycle? Do they seem to be in any one particular place on the mud flats?

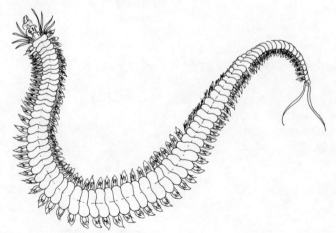

Clam worm (Nereis)

Another place to find nereids is in their burrows. At low tide you can see small holes in the mud surrounded by piles of sand balls and detritus called castings. These holes on the surface of the intertidal flats are the entrances to the worm burrows. Use a fork to investigate the burrows since it causes less damage than a trowel.

Observing Wandering Polychaetes. Gently dig around the burrow openings. Put the mud you collect onto a sieve (window screening will do nicely), and sift out the sand and mud particles. You may need to wash some sea water over the surface of your sieve. The worms will remain behind. While you dig, you may be able to trace the path of the burrow.

Some nereid worms will probably be among the array of creatures you have unearthed. *A Field Guide to the Atlantic Seashore* or another appropriate field guide will help you determine which of the many different kinds of worms you have captured. Put your polychaete into a flat container to which you have added some seawater. Observe it swimming. How does it use its body and its paddles to move?

How many segments does your worm have? Find some other worms of the same kind. Do they all have the same number of segments?

How many side feet, or paddles, does it have? How are they arranged on the worm's body? How do they feel? What is attached to the paddles? Use your hand lens for a better view.

Put enough sand in your container so that the worm can wriggle along on it. Do the paddles leave tracks? How are the tiny bristles helpful to the moving worm?

Is the worm flat or round? Is it the same color on the top as on the bottom?

How long is your worm? How wide is it? Watch the worm carefully as it moves about in your container. Does it get longer, thinner? How much longer?

Hold the worm gently but firmly behind its head and turn it so that the worm is facing you. How many pairs of tentacles do you see? What do you think they are used for?

Look for eyes. How many pairs do you find? Nereid eyes are designed to see only shades of light and dark. Why is this sufficient for the worm's lifestyle?

Gently press down on the surface of the worm. How does it feel?

Nereids are carnivores. Put a piece of fish in the container. How does the worm eat? How many "teeth" do you see?

When you have finished your observations, put your worm back onto the surface of the mud or sand where you found it. How long does it take to burrow? How will you know where to find a *Nereis* again?

Finding Sedentary Polychaetes. Stay-at-home cousins of the errant poly-chaetes are the sedentary polychaetes. These worms live most of their lives inside tubes that they build from a mix of sand and bits of broken shells glued together with mucus secreted by the worm. Some species are equipped with elaborate and very beautiful sets of plumes, which they wave gently in the water, capturing snippets of food as they drift in the current. With the aid of a face mask or a glass-bottom bucket, you can observe the worms feeding in the shallows of the intertidal zone. Make these observations while the tide is up. Among the most exquisite are the terebellid worms, which can be found from the Gulf of St. Lawrence to the tropics. With the help of your field guide, see how many different kinds you can find. Make a list of other creatures you find in the same area.

Another probable addition to your sedentary polychaete collection may be lugworms, which, like their *Nereis* relatives, are used extensively for fishing bait. You can spot the burrows of these worms by the coils or tiny balls heaped at one end of the burrow. Very close to these little piles you will notice small funnel-like depressions in the sand. The funnel is created by the worm as it

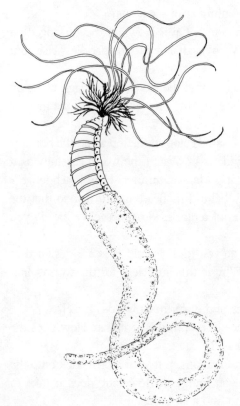

Terebellid worm

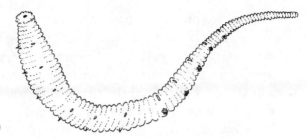

Lugworm (Arenicola)

gorges itself on the sand, which is rich in detritus, while the nonedible matter is excreted to form the castings on the surface of the mud.

The lugworm is also a mason. To prevent its burrow from collapsing, the worm structurally fortifies the walls with a mucous plaster it secretes. How many burrows can you find?

Capture a lugworm and put it in a flat plastic container with some seawater. Touch the worm body. How does it feel? Although this sedentary worm doesn't wander the flats in search of a meal, it still needs to move through its U-shaped burrow. The stiff bristles on its body give the worm leverage by grabbing into the sides of the burrow.

Alternative Methods for Finding Polychaete Worms. If you have difficulty finding worms in their habitats, you usually can get some at local bait and tackle shops.

EXPLORATIONS

Taking the Pulse of a Worm. Polychaetes live in an ever changing environment. You can discover how one of these environmental variables affects the worms by experimenting with changes in temperature. If you have not succeeded in capturing a mud worm, you can obtain a clam worm (also called a sandworm) in a bait shop. The clam worm, or *Nereis*, is a good subject for this investigation, because it is easy to observe the expansion and contraction of a blood vessel located along the back of the worm. The vessel appears as a dark, wavy line along the dorsal, or top, side of the worm as the vessel fills and expands; the vessel disappears under the skin when it contracts and empties. Thus the animal's pulse rate can be counted.

You may find that this counting requires careful observation through your hand lens and the extra light of a flashlight held close to the worm. You also may need a helper with a watch to count and time the beats as you call them out. To determine the pulse rate per minute, simply count the beats for fifteen seconds and multiply that number by four. The beat may be more obvious at the tail end of the worm.

What do you predict will happen to the animal's pulse rate if the temperature of the surrounding water is decreased? Increased? What strategies would the worm use to protect itself from the severe extremes of winter temperatures?

In order to control the temperature of your worm, find a spot in which to work that is out of direct sunlight, since you do not want the sun to interfere. Put a small amount of water and some chipped ice into a small Ziploc bag. After you have counted the pulse rate at room temperature, put your worm on the cold plastic bag and count again several times. You can test the effect of higher temperatures by adding warm water to a plastic bag. How is the pulse rate of the worm affected by temperature? When you're finished with the worm, be sure to return it to its habitat.

To continue your observations of polychaete worms, why not build a "worm-a-quarium"? Put about three inches of sandy mud into a large mayonnaise jar. Cover the mud with a sheet of waxed paper and pour seawater into the jar. Remove the waxed paper. The covering on the mud will prevent it from mixing with the water and making your system murky. To supply necessary oxygen to the water, you can buy a bubbler, a pump, and some plastic tubing from an aquarium supply shop at minimal cost. The equipment can be used again for other watery habitats that you might want to build. As you acquire marine worms, you can add them to the mini-habitat and make observations over a period of time.

PART III
THE BEACH

T HE BEACH CALLS to those seeking solitude or a brief respite from the struggles of life. It's a place to go where you can put problems aside and be refreshed by salt air and sea breezes. The beach is a curious place, for it is one of contrasts. It's the same, yet always changing; it belongs both to the land and to the sea. The sea both caresses the beach and unmercifully assaults it. The beach is a place of conflict, where powerful waves and currents tear away the land but also rebuild the land. It is a place of struggle between solid earth and liquid water. The sea builds the beach and tears it down; the sea molds the beach and is held back by the beach.

CHAPTER 15

The Sand

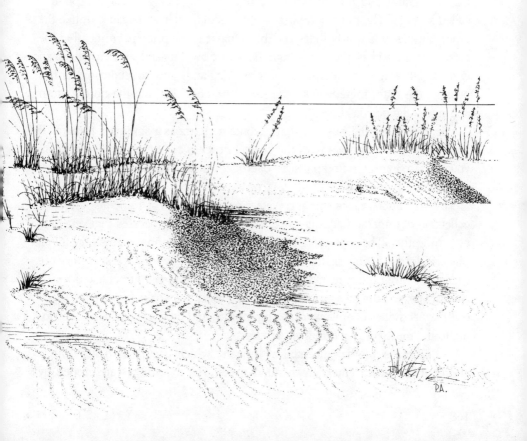

BOULDER BITS AND SPLINTERED SHELLS

Perhaps the most familiar characteristic of a beach is sand; and though all sandy beaches may look the same from a distance, they can actually be very different. For example, upon close examination, minerals such as the light tan feldspar and glistening quartz grains from the beaches of Long Island's south shore or New Jersey's shore contrast sharply with the stark white coral grains from the beaches of Florida and the Keys. Pick up a small handful of sand and look at it closely with a magnifier. What you see will depend very much on where you are, because sand is not one thing, but many things, which can be as different as oranges and bananas! In all sands you will probably see individual grains in a variety of colors, shapes, and sizes. If your sand sample is from a beach in the Northeast, those tiny particles, some perhaps millions of years old, have been eroded from granite and other igneous (fire born) rock formations. Because of the origin of the particles, you'll probably see fragments that look like tiny pieces of glass. With their sharp corners rounded from thousands of years of weathering, you are undoubtedly looking at quartz.

Quartz is created when the elements silicon and oxygen are bound together chemically under great heat and pressure. Quartz and other minerals found in granite, such as feldspar and mica, belong to a group of compounds called silicates. The mineral quartz is of particular interest, because unlike the other silicates, it is nearly indestructible. Quartz is the principal mineral in the earth's crust, and is the main ingredient of New England and Appalachian granite. Since it is so abundant in New England, and so enduring, it has become the main ingredient in the sandy beaches that line the northeastern and mid-Atlantic coastlines.

Beaches along the west coast, too, contain quartz as a dominant mineral. If you examine sand from any of the coastal beaches of Oregon or Washington, you can also expect to find particles of eroded volcanic rock; look for very dark grains mixed with the sparkling quartz.

By definition, rocks are aggregates, or collections, of minerals, and this collection of mineral matter is made into sand by two processes that generally occur together. The first process is mechanical weathering, or disintegration, physical forces acting on the rock. One of the weathering forces is pressure caused by rapid freezing and thawing of water that seeps into cracked rocks. Another force is the pressure exerted by tree roots that snake into crevices. The ordinary activities of ants, worms, chipmunks, and other rodents also contribute to the mechanical weathering process.

Abrasion is another mechanical process, which occurs as flakes, chips, and chunks of rock enter streams and rivers. The rock pieces are eroded by tumbling and grinding against boulders that line streambeds. Most of the sand found on the beaches of New England and along the mid-Atlantic coast was carried to the sea by rivers like the Merrimack in Massachusetts, the Connecticut, the Hudson in New York, the Delaware, the Susquehanna in Pennsylvania and Maryland, and the Pee Dee in the Carolinas.

The mighty Columbia River in the Pacific Northwest, which is itself fed by such major waterways as the Snake and the Willamette rivers, carries huge amounts of silt and mineral matter to the sea. Farther to the south, the Sacramento River rasps its watery tongue along a rocky bed and frees minerals for deposit on California's coastal beaches.

In areas where there are no rivers flowing from the mountains and no granite boulders along the shoreline to release tough quartz and shiny mica, the sand is very different in its composition. For instance, if you closely examined a handful of sand from the beaches of Florida or the Bahamas, you would find that it is not silicate sand; it is not made from sparkling particles of quartz. Instead, the sand is made from calcium carbonate from pulverized shells and coral and from the exoskeletons of tiny marine animals. This sand is usually almost white and feels softer than quartz sand. It owes its existence to the presence of abundant life in the sea. Over the millennia these little creatures have died, disintegrated, and been deposited by waves on coastal beaches.

Although about 90 percent of the sand on the New England and mid-Atlantic beaches is made of quartz, you will also find sparkling mica and the greenish black of hornblende. Purple garnet is found as well, but unfortunately, the large pieces usually turned into fine jewelry are not found on the beach. If you run a small magnet through the sand, you probably will remove bits of dark magnetite and ilmenite, which are iron bearing minerals found in some igneous and metamorphic rocks. Additional colors, such as tan, pink, and green, that you find in some sands are determined by other minerals released from the parent rocks. For example, the black sands of some of our beaches in the Pacific Northwest speak to their volcanic origin, while green particles, often indicating glauconite (found on the ocean floor), are brought to beaches by offshore currents. Since the minerals that make up sand are of different weights, they are occasionally sorted by wind and waves, leaving many beaches streaked with their colors.

Not all beaches are sandy. Some beaches are made up of shell fragments from local mollusks. Oyster shell beaches are common in some areas. There are also clam shell beaches and mussel beaches. These beaches are not too inviting for stretching out a towel and lying in the sun. They are usually found in a protected area of shore where the shells are not pounded by wave action into fine calcium carbonate sand. Beaches can be classified according to the material that forms them. (See Chapter Note 3 for the Wentworth grain size scale.) The beaches on Cape Ann, Massachusetts, and others that pepper the shores of Penobscot Bay in Maine are made from boulders deposited by the last glacier of the Pleistocene. Other beaches, especially common along the New England coast, are made from cobbles, which are round, melon-sized stones. A fine example of a cobble beach can be found near Point Judith, Rhode Island. Here, listening to the clacking of cobbles as they slam against each other in the backwash of retreating waves, you can witness one tiny step in the process of sand production. Other beaches are formed of smaller stones and may be called gravel, or pebble, beaches. These beaches are common where wave action erodes the glacial deposits known as terminal moraines. Typical gravel beaches are found along the north shore of Long Island.

Extremely fine sand can be found along part of the Florida coast. For example, the sand at Daytona Beach is so fine that it packs firmly enough for automobiles to drive along its length. Yet farther up the Florida coast, conditions are quite different. You won't find cars on that stretch of beach, since the sand particles are larger and cannot be packed so closely together. The vehicles would sink up to their hubcaps in the relatively soft sand.

While weathered rock, broken shell fragments, and organic matter are among the primary building materials of beaches, waves and wind are the architects that build and reshape the beach. Storm waves formed thousands of miles out at sea contain tremendous amounts of energy, which is released when they impact on the beach. Under very turbulent conditions, they can bring a load of sand, gathered from the ocean bottom offshore or from another area of the beach, and deposit it. In the process of depositing their baggage, the waves also sort sand grains, leaving the finer grains of sand toward the top, or landward edge, of the beach. The heavier, larger material is deposited near the water's edge or carried away. In the backwash (the water that retreats from the beach), the larger sand grains may be ground finer as they are dragged back into the sea. This process is carried on by every wave that hits the beach. Since ocean currents run parallel to the beach in most places, the waves are constantly moving the sand along the beach.

So it is that each receding wave carries away sand for deposition at some distant point. If the amount of sand deposited is equal to that taken away, the beach will remain unchanged. However, since this perfect balance probably never occurs, a beach is always shrinking or growing. This process is dramatically accelerated by storms. When we visit a beach following a hurricane, we are only seeing the slow process greatly speeded up. Communities often spend a great deal of energy and money trying to stop the cycle of erosion and deposition by building expensive barriers and rock groins or jetties. A look at the history of our coastline tells us that these structures only serve to delay the inevitable process of change. Man is not the architect of the beach; he can only build his sandcastles and watch what the ocean will do.

THE WORLD OF SAND

What you will need

basic kit
camera
small baby food jars with lids
sheets of plastic
vinegar
string or clothesline
flashlight

Science skills

observing
graphing
inferring
measuring

OBSERVATIONS

Making a Collection of Beaches. Beaches are especially interesting to study because they come in such great variety. Most people who travel like to get off the beaten track and visit beaches. Instead of just looking at the beaches, you can "collect" them by making careful observations and some simple sketches or photographs. You will find that beaches only a few miles apart can be very different and that they can change from year to year and even from season to season within the same year.

The Parts of a Beach. Beaches are defined by one scientist (see Hoyt in the Bibliography) as "those areas that form between the highest point on land to which waves deposit rock pieces of various sizes and the outer breaking waves." Included in this definition are the foreshore, or the area between high and low tide, and the berm, which is the section of the beach marking the highest limit of storm wave action. Going inland from the berm, the area called the back beach slopes slightly downward. This back beach, only rarely touched by wave action, ends at the foot of the first row of dunes. With the help of the diagram below, compare the structure of your beach with that of the "typical beach."

Recording the Variations. Is the slope of the foreshore steep or gradual? Is the berm wide or narrow? Observe the wave action. Wave height is determined by the vertical distance between the top (crest) of the wave and the bottom (trough). You can see wave structure in the illustration below. Can you estimate the approximate height of the waves offshore? Do they break close to the beach

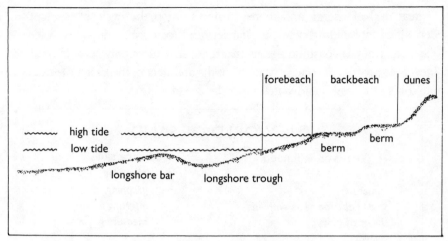

Profile of a sandy beach

or out some distance from shore? In your notebook, identify the name and location of the beach. Be sure to include the weather conditions and the date of your observations.

Write a description of your beach that includes its color and the size and texture of the sand particles that make it up. Are the size and texture of the particles uniform throughout the beach from the water's edge at low tide to the splash zone? If the particle size is not uniform, how is it different? Is the slope in the foreshore steep or is it gradual? What is the relationship between the slope of the beach and the size of sand particles? Take a picture that will show the parts of the beach.

A Comparison between Beaches. Go to another beach, preferably during the same season and under the same weather conditions as in the previous exercise. How do the beaches compare? Is the foreshore steeper or more gradual? Is the berm of the second beach wider, narrower, or the same as the berm of your first beach? Is the back beach wider or narrower? Observe the wave action. Are the waves larger, smaller, or about the same? What is the relationship between wave height and the slope of the beach? (See Chapter Note 1 for an idea on this subject.) What is the relationship between slope and grain size? Don't forget to make a record of this beach in your notebook as you did before.

Seasonal Changes. Since beaches change from day to day and from season to season, they are considered dynamic. To find out how and to what extent beaches are changed by winter storms and the relative calm of summer waves, compare your beaches during the summer and winter. Photograph them throughout the year if you can. Explain the differences you observe. Did winter storms invade the back beach? Was sand removed and the beach profile remolded? Pay attention to wind direction. In summer the prevailing winds on the east coast of the United States are often from the southwest, while in the winter they are from the northwest. On the northwest coast the prevailing winds are often variable but generally from the west throughout the year. Consult local newspapers for precise information. What do you predict will be the effect of such changes on the size and shape of the foreshore and on the dunes?

EXPLORATIONS

The Sizes of Sand Particles. Among the factors that make a beach unique is the sand found there. Observe the sand from different areas of the beach, such as the foreshore, the berm, and the back beach. (See the diagram.) What is the relationship between particle size and the distance from the water's edge? (See Chapter Note 2 for a brief explanation.) What is the relationship between the slope of the beach and particle size? (Use the Wentworth scale in Chapter Note 3 to determine particle size.) What are some of the generalizations you can make about the size of the sand particles and their location on the beach?

A Sand Sample Collection. You can study more than the size of sand grains on each beach. You can add actual sand samples to your collection of facts. Clean baby food jars with lids make ideal collecting bottles. Label each jar with the date, the location of the beach, and the part of the beach the sand came from. You will also want to include the wave action, such as the wave height and time between waves breaking on the shore. Some of the sand you collect will need to be washed with fresh water to remove particles of silt and bits of organic debris. Dry the sand by spreading it on sheets of plastic. Be sure to label the drying sheets to avoid a mix-up when you return each sample to its container.

If your friends travel to coastal regions different from the places you visit, ask them to bring you a small sample of sand from those beaches. Be sure you tell them how to label the collecting jars. This is a good way for you to get sand from beaches along the Atlantic and Pacific coasts as well as from the Gulf of Mexico.

Identifying Sand Types. Depending on its origin, sand can be divided into two groups. If it comes from the breakdown of animal skeletons, shells of mollusks, bits of coral, and pieces of sea urchin spines, it is referred to as biological sand. If the sand is the result of weathering and erosion of rocks, it is called nonbiological sand. Put about one-half teaspoon of sand on a piece of dark colored paper and examine it with a hand lens. What shapes and colors are the sand grains? What size are the sand particles? (See the grain size chart in Chapter Note 3.) Are the grains flat? Do they have sharp edges? Are there bits and pieces of shells in the sample? Are there grains of different colors? What minerals do you think are in the sand sample? Use the field guide suggested in the Bibliography to identify the minerals you might find.

Calcium Carbonate Sand. Biological sands contain animal remains, such as crab carapaces, mollusk shells, and sea urchin spines. These exoskeletons are made of calcium carbonate. To find out whether or not your sand has biological origins, put a few drops of vinegar on a pinch of sand. Calcium carbonate will react with acidic vinegar by forming bubbles of carbon dioxide. Since nonbiological sand will contain some calcium carbonate particles, you must observe this reaction closely with your hand lens. Are only a few particles reacting with the vinegar or is the reaction a general reaction among almost all the sand particles?

A COLLECTION OF LIVING THINGS AT THE BEACH

The Strand Line. A line of debris often runs parallel to the water's edge, marking the line of high tide. Commonly called a wrack line, or strand line, it is made of material that's been "stranded" by tidal waters or storm waves. The strand line contains materials that once floated in the sea, carried by winds and currents. This debris may have traveled only a few miles or it may have journeyed several thousands of miles from its place of origin.

Sampling the Strand Line. Walk along the strand line of your beach and examine its contents at regular intervals, every ten feet or so. Make a tally sheet of everything you find in it. Sort the material into groups. Do you have anything that is of human origin such as Styrofoam cups, plastic plates, pieces of rope, or fishing line? Are there any signs of animal life, like shells, egg cases,

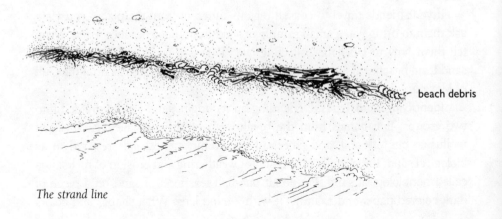

beach debris

The strand line

or crab or lobster sheds? Is there any evidence of plant life, such as driftwood or eelgrass (*Zostera marina*)? Do you find a variety of seaweeds? Does one particular type of seaweed seem to predominate?

With the help of the field guides suggested in the Bibliography, identify the various objects that you found in the strand line. What did you find most often? What was rarely found? Which of your groups had the most material? Which had the least? Transfer this information to a chart and see if you can find any relationships.

Beach Zonation. Although zonation is much less obvious on the beach than in other intertidal habitats, bands of life exist from mean high water to mean low water. Tide, salinity, exposure, and the shifting of the sand affect what organisms are found. So that your exploration of the intertidal beach is not haphazard, use the method described below to discover the variety of life and its distribution in the beach habitat.

Make a transect by laying a string or a clothesline from the splash zone (see illustration) to the water's edge, securing each end of the line with a rock or

TALLY SHEET OF
OBJECTS FOUND IN STRAND LINE

Name of Beach:
Location:
Date:

Recent Weather
Conditions:

What Was Found	Approximate Number at Each Station				
Slipper shells					
Seaweed types					
a) *Ulva*					
b) *Chondrus crispus*					
Skate egg cases					
Whelk egg cases					
Plastic					
Styrofoam					
Nylon fishing line					
Miscellaneous					
Station Every Ten Feet	10	20	30	40	50

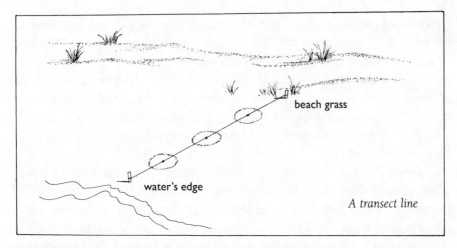

beach grass

water's edge

A transect line

other heavy object. Tie knots at regular intervals along this line. With a knot as its center, you can scribe a circle in the sand using a piece of string six inches long. Do this at each knot, so that you will have a series of circles, each with a diameter of twelve inches. If you prefer, you can use a wire coat hanger to form the circles, placing it at each knot as you work your way down the transect line.

Beginning at the top of the splash zone, examine each of the circles along the transect by carefully digging up the sand to look for any living things that might be there. Spread the sand onto a flat sheet of plastic, gently separating the particles. What do you find? Dig deeper. What do you find at this new depth? At each circle along the transect, examine the sand and dig to the same depth as you did before. Keep a record of what you find and how many of each living thing there are in each location. Where did you find the greatest number and greatest variety of living things and where did you find the least? How do you explain your findings? Use your field guide to identify the living things you found.

Beach Fleas. A common inhabitant of the strand line is the beach flea, from the *Orchestia* genus. These agile tan or olive scavengers feed on decaying

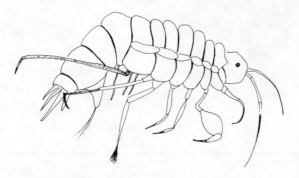

Beach flea
(Gammarus talorchestia)

plant and animal material. They transform enormous amounts of algae into protein, which is used by members of higher trophic (energy) levels, such as the shore birds that feed on them. When captured and examined with the aid of a hand lens, beach fleas look like tiny shrimp and show many of the characteristics of amphipods, including jointed legs and segmented bodies. How many body segments can you find? How many legs?

The California beach flea (*Orchestoidea californiana*) reaches the spectacular size of one inch. If you are beachcombing on the west coast, capture one and answer the questions above. Another quite famous west coast creature is the "greedy" isopod, *Cirolana harfordi*. Watch these scavengers as they remove meat from dead fish and you'll know how they got their common name.

A different species of beach fleas is *Talorchestia*. Filling a different niche, they are active at night when they feed on beach wrack. If you spread a dark sheet of plastic near the strand line and place a lighted lantern on the plastic, you can coax them into captivity. Since many of your captives will be one and one-half inches or more in length, a bug box is a good place to observe them. How many legs do they have? What is the shape of the body? How are they different from the other group of beach hoppers? What do you think dines on these fleas of the night?

Ghost Crabs. Relatives of the fiddler crabs, these agile beach animals have the formidable name of *Ocypode quadrata*. They scurry around the sand of the upper beach at night on shores from Rhode Island to Texas. Often the only sign of their presence is a hole in the sand that marks the entrance to their burrows. Their tunnels into the sand can reach a depth of four feet.

Ghost crabs remain beneath the sand during the heat of the day and venture out only at dusk, at night, and at dawn. Since their colors very closely match those of the sand, ghost crabs are very difficult to see as they run across the beach in search of a meal. With the help of a flashlight and some fancy footwork, you should be able to capture one of these crabs. See if you can discover how they are adapted to life in the upper beach. (See Chapter Note 4 for some of these adaptations.)

Ghost crab
(Ōcypode quadrata)

Scientists who have studied animal life on a large number of beaches tell us that there is a direct negative correlation between the number of ghost crabs on a beach and the degree of human interference. The more human activity there is on a beach, the fewer the number of ghost crabs. What are the ghost crabs "telling" you about the presence of people on your beach?

Ghost crabs have a varied diet. Based on your observations, what role do these animals have in food chains? (See Chapter Note 5 for some information on crab dietary preferences.)

Mole Crabs. As you sit at the edge of the water watching the waves dash up to your feet and scurry back over the swash zone, you may eventually spot the elusive mole crab. This fascinating member of the mid-Atlantic beach community makes its home in this most unstable, turbulent habitat, where few animals and no plants can exist. The male mole crab is only one-half inch long; the female is about one inch long. They are egg shaped, and have the color and texture of an egg. They have no pincer claws, and the legs and other parts fold flat against the body. When they feed, they dig in the lower part of their bodies facing away from the waves. They lie low as the wave washes up the foreshore, but then they extend their feathery antennae when the thin sheet of water flows back over them. The antennae capture very tiny bits of food from the rushing water. They occasionally move across the wet sand as the tide moves the swash zone up or down the foreshore. When you attempt to capture one, it will dig itself out of sight in a flash. The mole crabs (*Emerita*) are a delight to watch; luckily they can be found along the swash zones from Alaska to Peru and from Cape Cod, Massachusetts, to Florida and Texas. How many special adaptations to their special beach niche can you identify? (See Chapter

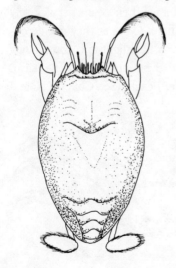

Mole crab

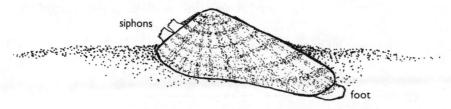

siphons

foot

Coquina clam (Donax variabilis)

Note 6 for some of these adaptations.) Shore birds prey upon this hardy little surf dweller.

Coquina Clams. Although the tiny coquina clam *(Donax variabilis)* is only about one-half inch across, it is very active. On the high-energy sandy beaches south of Cape Hatteras on the Atlantic coast, you will not find any mole crabs. Instead, you will find the coquina clam. You might find a few coquinas as far north as the beaches of Delaware. The coquina feeds the same way that the mole crab does. It uses its strong foot to move up and down the beach with the tide, so that it stays in the swash zone. Like the mole crab, it is a filter feeder, feeding as the wave washes back down the sand. It can dig into the sand very quickly. You will be surprised at the great variety of colors and patterns that mark the coquina shell.

Food Chains on the Beach. What role do beach fleas, ghost crabs, coquina clams, and mole crabs play in beach food chains? Are they predators, scavengers? What evidence did you use to make your decision? Based on your observations of this and other beach food chains, construct a beach food web. Don't forget about the animals you discovered living along your transect.

CHAPTER NOTES

1. Slope of the Foreshore. If a beach has a very gradual slope in the swash zone where the waves hit the beach, the waves dissipate their energy in movement up the beach. The larger waves sweep farther up the beach. If the swash zone is steep, if it has a steep pitch, the waves tend to crash with great force onto the sand without much forward motion. This beach is called a high-energy beach. This kind of beach can be very dangerous for surfing or swimming.

2. Sand Particle Size and Location. The coarser the sand, the closer it is to the water's edge. Light particles can be carried farther up the beach by wind and water transport. On a gently sloping beach, the backwash has considerably less energy than the oncoming wave; therefore it carries relatively little sand away from the beach. In contrast, the backwash on a steep beach has a great deal of energy and removes not only large amounts of sand but cobbles, as well.

3. Wentworth Grain Size Scale.

WENTWORTH GRAIN SIZE SCALE

	Wentworth Size Description	Diameter	Average Beach Slope
	Boulder	>256 mm	>25°
GRAVEL	Cobble	65–256 mm	19–23°
GRAVEL	Pebble	4–64 mm	13–19°
GRAVEL	Granule	2–4 mm	11°
SAND	Very Coarse Sand	1–2 mm	9°
SAND	Coarse Sand	.5–1 mm	7°
SAND	Medium Sand	.25–.5 mm	5°
SAND	Fine Sand	.07–.25 mm	<5°
MUD	Silt	.003–.07 mm	0°
MUD	Clay	<.003 mm	Particles often wash away with rain and waves

4. **Ghost Crab Adaptations.** Some ghost crab adaptations to the upper beach include thick, bristle-like structures near the gill openings, very long antennae, and a waterproof carapace. The "bristles" help keep sand from interfering with gill function and help prevent water loss when the crab has been left high and dry by the falling tide. The long antennae can remove pesky sand grains from crab eyes. The carapace is almost impermeable, which prevents excessive water loss.

5. **The Diet of the Ghost Crab.** Ghost crabs, like other crabs, are predators. They seem to prefer mole crabs and bean clams (coquina clams). However, a snack of dead fish and the remains of other animals will do in a pinch.

6. **Mole Crab Adaptations.** Some mole crab adaptations for successfully living in the zone of mean low water include short, strong legs and a telson that acts like a shovel for a quick, rear-end-first getaway into wet sand. A very smooth carapace is ideal for slipping effortlessly into the safety of a burrow. Specially designed antennae are for the removal of wet, sticky sand grains from the eyes.

CHAPTER 16

Sand Dunes

SILENT SENTINELS

Dune fields transmit a special feeling, a mystical quality. On a January day, the somber mood of these brooding places is punctuated by the piercing steel knife of an icy wind and by the screams of a few gulls that scribe circles in the sky overhead. Only by walking among the dunes, sheltered in the swales between them, are you warmed by the winter sun. There the shrieking winds, blown fresh from the sea, are reduced to gentle moans and carry the promise of the spring yet to come.

Born of sea, sand, and wind, extensive dune systems occur most frequently along the beaches of the barrier islands that stretch intermittently along our coastline. The wide and gently sloping continental shelf contributes considerable amounts of sand to the construction of these dunes. Washed onto the beach by the sea, the sand dries, accumulates, and is moved around by the wind. When the sand-laden wind meets an object such as a piece of driftwood or other debris, it slows down and drops some of its freight of fine sand. Grain piles on top of grain, and slowly a small sand mound builds. From this meager beginning, the wind, a skillful artisan, crafts the dune. As the pile of sand increases in height and width, it offers more resistance to the wind, and a steady supply of new sand for the developing dune is guaranteed.

Sand carried up a newly formed hill falls over the crest and gives the emerging dune its characteristic shape. The windward side of the dune (the side facing the wind) develops a gradual slope, while the leeward side of the maturing dune (the side away from the wind) becomes quite steep.

The first line of dunes that develops landward of the beach, generally behind the strand line, is called the primary dune. Exposed to wind, salt spray, and extreme temperature changes, the arid primary dunes are inhospitable toward living things except for the sand-holding grasses, beach heather (*Hudsonia tomentosa*), and other hardy pioneers.

In the windshade on the lee side of the primary dune, wind velocity decreases, sand movement slows, salt spray is diminished, and a line of

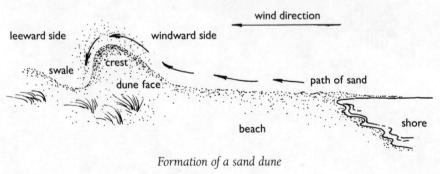

Formation of a sand dune

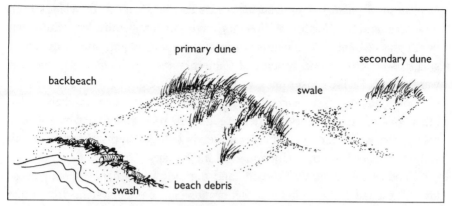

Dune sequence

secondary dunes develops. If the ridges of the primary and secondary dunes are parallel to each other, a swale, or hollow, forms between them. Swales, sheltered from the winds, are often close enough to the water table so that a bog or marsh community develops in them. Wild cranberries, blue irises, and delicate orchids can be found in these wet regions of Atlantic coast dune swales. Those swales lacking such surface water become basins that catch falling sand as it blows over the crests of the primary dunes. It is in this habitat that you'll find seaside goldenrod, beach pea, beach plums, and wild cherries.

Dune formation is subject to the vagaries of wind speed and direction, as well as sand supply. Therefore, if you visit any of the dune fields on Canada's Prince Edward Island, the dunes along the beaches of southern Maine or Long Island, the dunes on the barrier beaches of the Carolinas, or the extensive dune system of the Pacific Northwest, you'll notice that dunes come in a variety of shapes and sizes. Perhaps you will also find a maritime forest with stubby oaks and pitch pines that have been pruned by salt spray, along with hardy perennial shrubs, growing behind the line of secondary dunes.

If the dune remains free of plant life, or if existing vegetation dies, strong winds will gradually blow the dune inland. These nonvegetated sand hills begin to "walk" in the direction of the prevailing winds. Such marauding dunes have been known to travel as much as sixty feet in one year. On their landward journey, they have engulfed lighthouses, trees, buildings, and other objects that happened to be in their way. Years later the buried obstacles have emerged as the gypsy dunes continued their nomadic life. Still other nonvegetated sand hills have "wandered" across highways, covering them overnight to the extent that snowplows were needed to remove the sand.

Most dunes don't travel like this; they become stabilized by plant life. One of the primary plants in dune stabilization is American beach grass (*Am-*

mophila breviligulata). This tenacious grass can be found in dunelands from Newfoundland to North Carolina. Its environmental equivalent, European beach grass *(Ammophila arenaria)* thrives on Cape Cod and also in the much smaller west coast dune systems of California and Washington. On the seaward edge of Pacific coast dunes, you'll find wild rye grass *(Elymus mollis)* and seashore bluegrass *(Poa macrantha)* among the primary dune stabilizers. Like other grasses, these develop extensive fibrous root systems, which firmly anchor the plants. Seashore bluegrass sends out side roots about fifteen to eighteen inches from the plant and eight inches deep.

Another gold medal winner in sand trapping is sea oats *(Uniola paniculata).* These tall grasses, often five feet or more, grace dune systems from Cape Henry, Virginia, to Texas. Sea oats are vigorous and stubborn. Like the beach grasses, they've been provided with wonderful adaptations, so that they can endure the harsh life in the primary dune, including extremes in temperature, salt spray, intense sunlight, high velocity winds, and water-starved sand.

Beneath its plume-like flower heads and thin, light stem that gently sways in the sea breezes, a water-seeking tap root stretches six feet or deeper into the ground. Like the beach grasses, sea oats send out underground stems called rhizomes, which develop fibrous root systems known to reach several feet into the sand in search of water. In addition, the nodes (swellings along the rhi-

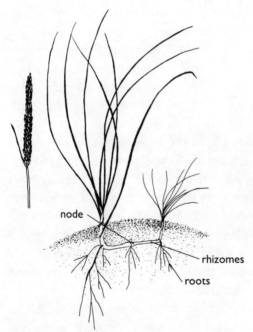

Beach grass (Amophilis breviligulata)

Sea oats (Uniola paniculata)

zomes) produce new aerial shoots. These tiny new shoots pierce the surface of the sand and begin the job of slowing the wind and snaring the sand it carries. Sea oats also produce seeds that ripen in the late summer and are carried away by the wind, thus spreading the plant to new locations.

Beach grass has a curious relationship with a nonliving component in its environment that makes it particularly valuable as a dune-sand stabilizer. The grass not only thrives in this sandy world, but actually requires sand to stimulate root production. This activity yields more plants to trap sand, thus paving the way for other beach plants that can thrive in this gritty environment.

A sandy habitat also benefits sea oats. Research suggests that the sand insulates the plant against excessive heat and prevents water loss from its delicate tissues. In addition, laboratory investigations have shown that sea oats have the unique ability to obtain some of their nutritional requirements from dissolved minerals carried in salt spray.

Sea oats and beach grass are often seen together where their ranges overlap, from southeastern Virginia to northeastern North Carolina. Beach grass flourishes when the average daily temperature is about seventy to eighty degrees Fahrenheit. At higher temperatures, the grass seems unable to manufacture food. Since sea oats are semitropical plants, they thrive in warmer climates and are intolerant of severe winters; but when it comes to drought, sea oats have the competitive edge.

Coastal communities and conservation groups have become aware of the value of sand dunes. We now know that stable dune fields protect the land behind them from abusive salt spray, onshore winds, and the ravages of winter storms. Dune management programs and science research groups have been working together to help protect these very important natural resources. In some states, sand dunes and sea oats (*Uniola*) are protected by law.

We must treasure our dunes, and in return, they will enrich our environment. They will also enrich the thoughtful beach visitor with their quiet, ephemeral beauty.

THE WORLD OF SAND DUNES

What you will need
basic kit
trowel
tape
camera
thermometers
string or clothesline
wire clothes hanger
long pole

Science skills
observing
measuring
graphing
explaining
inferring

OBSERVATIONS

Observing a Dune System. To begin your observations of a dune system, find a place where you can get an overview of the dune field. You will notice that the sequence of these sand hills is more or less parallel to the water's edge. You will also observe that the vegetation from the foredune landward is arranged in horizontal bands, or zones, that are distinguished by changes in plant color from light to dark green and by changes in plant density from sparsely settled to thickly vegetated. How many zones do you see?

A Typical Foredune. The first row of dunes back from the beach are the primary dunes. What shape are they? Round? Pointed? Steep-sided? Symmetrical or asymmetrical? Now observe the foredune, or face of the primary dune. Are there any plants growing on the foredune? How many different kinds of plants do you find?

Draw a picture or take a photograph that shows the pattern of plant life on the primary dunes.

Is there a relationship between the shape of the dunes and the direction of the prevailing winds? How does the shape of the windward side of the foredune differ from that of the leeward side? How does the plant life differ on the leeward and windward sides of the dune?

Beach Grass. Beach grass, like sea oats, contributes to the stabilization of the dunes in a purely mechanical way. Look around the base of a beach grass plant and you will see the developing mound of sand. When the speed of sand-laden wind is reduced by the blades of grass or sea oats, the wind drops its baggage of tiny sand grains, which then settle around the base of the plants. The sand continues to collect, and its presence in moderate amounts stimulates the growth of beach grass and sea oats. The accumulating sand insulates the young plants against excessive heat and prevents them from drying out.

Finding the Parent Plant. Although many of the beach grass plants appear to be scattered randomly in the sand, you probably have discovered among them beach grass plants growing in a line of three or more across the sand dune. The first in this line of plants is the parent, distinguished from the offspring by its greater size. The shorter, younger plants in the line are those that have sprouted from rhizomes or underground stems. To get a good look at this method of asexual vegetative reproduction, carefully dig along the line of plants. How are the plants connected to one another? Identify the parent plant. How many offspring are there? What is the greatest distance between offspring? What is the total distance from the parent to the most recent plant? Find other parent grass plants and the offspring. Compare them as you did with the first plant. Do you find any similarities or differences between these sets of plants? Does asexual reproduction appear to be a common method of producing new plants? When you finish examining the plants, replace the disturbed sand. Never take any samples of beach grasses.

If you are visiting the dune fields of the Pacific Northwest, you might want to try this exercise with a line of big-headed sedge (*Carex macroencephala*), as well as with west coast dune grasses. These include wild rye grass and sea-shore bluegrass.

Beach Grass Adaptations. Beach grass has evolved many adaptations in order to thrive in this porous, dry habitat. One of these adaptations helps the grass to adjust to wide fluctuations in temperature and humidity. Observe the grass leaves on a hot, sunny day. Look at them early in the morning and again later the same day, perhaps an hour or two after noon. What differences do you observe in the leaves? In the cool of the evening, return to your plant. What differences in the leaves do you observe this time? Why does this happen?

In a previous activity, you have examined the root system of beach grass. How does this adaptation aid the plant's survival?

Sea Oats Adaptations. Sea oats, another dune-building plant, also has adaptations that ensure its survival in this exposed, hot, and dry habitat. Find some sea oats and dig gently around the plant. What type of root systems do

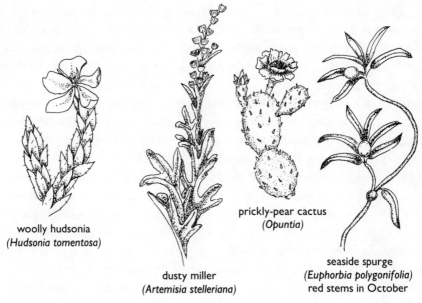

woolly hudsonia
(*Hudsonia tomentosa*)

prickly-pear cactus
(*Opuntia*)

dusty miller
(*Artemisia stelleriana*)

seaside spurge
(*Euphorbia polygonifolia*)
red stems in October

Plants of the dunes

these grasses have? Do sea oats survive the winter? What happens to them during the cold months?

In addition to underground stems, what other method does this grass have of spreading itself? Although the sea oat is forgiving of winter winds and stinging sand, it is unable to tolerate human interference, so be careful where you walk when exploring sand dunes. (See Chapter Note 1 for a brief explanation of sea oat adaptations.)

Other Plants Found on the Primary Dune. Some other plants found on the foredune are wooly hudsonia (*Hudsonia tomentosa*), dusty miller (*Artemisia stelleriana*), seaside goldenrod (*Solidago sempervirens*), beach pea (*Lathyrus japonicus*), and seaside spurge (*Euphorbia polygonifolia*). A field guide, such as *The Beachcomber's Botany*, will help you identify these and other members of the dune plant community. As you continue to explore the dunes, you'll probably be able to discover the clever tricks that these and other plants have perfected to survive the harsh environment of the dune fields. (See Chapter Note 2 for some of their strategies.)

If you are visiting west coast dune systems, look for beach silver-top (*Glehnia leiocarpa*), sandwort (*Honkenya peploides*), beach pea (*Lathyrus* sp.), and beach morning glory (*Convolvulus soldanella*). You will also find sea rocket (*Cakile maritima*), which grows on the east coast dunes, as well. Research has shown that sea rocket seedlings need the high intensity light found on a naked

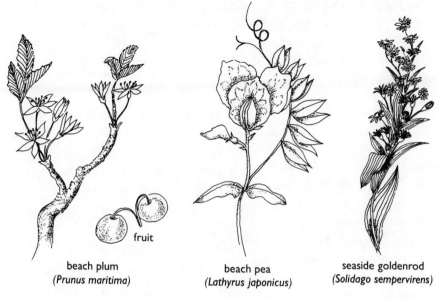

| beach plum | beach pea | seaside goldenrod |
| (*Prunus maritima*) | (*Lathyrus japonicus*) | (*Solidago sempervirens*) |

fruit

More plants of the dunes

dune. Apparently, sea rocket does not grow well in the shadow of other grasses or plants.

Make a list of the plants you find in the dune system and indicate their various strategies for survival. Look at the leaves and stems. How are these designed to protect the plants from the hot, drying sun, salt spray, and cold nights?

EXPLORATIONS

How Hot Is Hot? If you have ever walked barefoot on the beach on a hot summer day, you know that the sand can get very hot; you also know that by early evening the sand feels quite cool. How hot does the sand get during the day? Does it get hotter in some places in the dune fields than in others? Use a thermometer to measure the temperature of the sand on the front of the primary dune, the back of the primary dune, in the swale, and on the front and back of the secondary dune. You will need to begin early in the morning so that you can get a complete pattern of temperature variation during the day. (You can damage your thermometer if its range is too narrow, so be sure that it reads to one hundred degrees centigrade.) You should take several temperature readings in each location and find the average. At hourly intervals throughout the day, repeat the procedure. To avoid confusion, each location should have a separate data sheet similar to the one on page 192. In the evening when you

SURVIVAL STRATEGIES OF PLANTS LIVING IN A DUNE SYSTEM ON THE ATLANTIC COAST

Plants	Adaptations
• Beach heather (*Hudsonia tomentosa*)	
• Dusty miller (*Artemisia stelleriana*)	
• Cocklebur (*Xanthium echinatum*)	
• Sea rocket (*Cakile endentula*)	
• Seaside spurge (*Euphorbia polygonifolia*)	
• Seaside goldenrod (*Solidago sempervirens*)	
• Others	
•	
•	
•	

Date:

Location:

have finished, you can put your information for each location on a separate graph. This will show you the relationship between the time of the day and the temperature in each of the above places in the dune field. How do the temperatures change during the day? Do they change proportionally from one region to another? Does one area get disproportionately hot during the day? How do you explain these temperature variations? (See Chapter Note 3 for brief statements on temperature variations.)

Plant Variety in the Dunes. As you have observed, plant species in the dune fields grow in zones, which are determined by such factors as temperature fluctuations and exposure to wind and salt spray. How does the variety of plant species in the dune field change as the distance from the water-and-salt-laden wind increases? One way to find out is to make a transect across the dunes by laying a clothesline from the beach to the back of the secondary dunes. Then use a wire hanger or a piece of rope to make a square three feet by

SURVIVAL STRATEGIES OF PLANTS LIVING IN A DUNE SYSTEM ON THE PACIFIC COAST

Plants	Adaptations
• Beach silver-top (*Glehnia leiocarpa*)	
• Sandwort (*Honkenya peploides*)	
• Beach pea (*Lathyrus japonicus*)	
• Yarrow (*Achillea millefolium*)	
• Black beach knotweed (*Polygonum paryonchia*)	
• Beach morning glory (*Convolvulus soldanella*)	
• Others	
•	
•	
•	

Date:

Location:

three feet. This is a quadrat, which is simply a rigid square of any convenient size. The device is used by scientists to reduce large study areas into manageable plots.

To sample plant life in your dune system, lay the quadrat across the clothesline every five feet or at any other workable, regular interval. Begin at the face of the primary dune and follow your transect landward. Each time you lay your square on the transect, record the number of plant species in it. You will also want to record the number of individual plants of each species in the quadrat. Which plant type is most dense? (Density is the number of plants per unit area; your unit area is the size of your quadrat, or one square yard.) Which plant is least dense in each quadrat?

As you progress from the foredune to the back of a secondary dune, how does the variety of plant life change? Is there a greater number of different plant types? Where is the variety of plant life the greatest? Where is variety the

A LIST OF WEATHER CONDITIONS ON THE FOREDUNE AT HOURLY INTERVALS

Time*	Temperature	Wind Speed (Slight, None, Moderate, or Stiff)	Wind Direction
9 A.M.			
10 A.M.			
11 A.M.			
12 A.M.			
1 P.M.			
2 P.M.			
3 P.M.			
4 P.M.			
5 P.M.			
6 P.M.			
7 P.M.			
8 P.M.			

Location:

Date:

Weather Conditions:

*Begin your study earlier in the day if you are able to do so.

least? Are some plant species found in all of the quadrats? Do you find any sea oats or beach grass on the back of the secondary dune?

Vertical Zonation. As you have discovered, plant communities in the dune fields occur in a pattern of bands called plant zones. Another type of zonation occurs in the dunes to which animals have adapted. This is a vertical zonation, caused primarily by temperature variations above and below the sand.

Temperatures below the Sand. Take the temperature of the surface sand in a swale. Now dig into the sand about two inches and find the temperature in the hole. Continue digging in four-inch increments, taking the temperature at each four-inch depth until you've dug a hole about two feet deep. How did the temperature change as you dug into the sand? What are the implications of your findings for animal life in the dunes? Why is there an apparent absence of animals on the surface of the sand during the day?

TEMPERATURE VARIATION ON THE FOREDUNE DURING A TWELVE-HOUR PERIOD

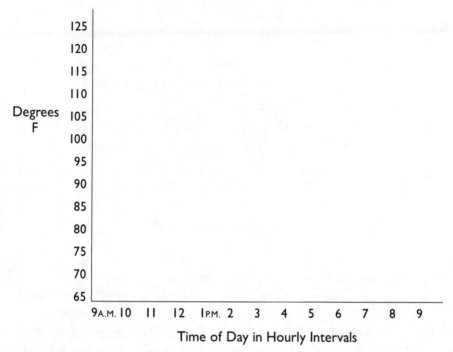

Time of Day in Hourly Intervals

Name of Beach:

Location:

Date:

Temperatures above the Sand. How does the temperature of the air change at increasing distances above the sand? To find out you will need a long pole; a broom handle will do. You will also need some additional thermometers to make the job a little easier for yourself. Tape the thermometers at regular intervals along the pole, beginning several inches from the bottom. Stick the pole, with its thermometers, into the ground. If you can only find one thermometer, the job will go a little more slowly, since you will have to remove and retape the thermometer after each reading.

What happens to the temperature of the air as the distance above the sand increases? Chart your results and be sure to include the time of day, the wind speed, the humidity, the color of the sand, and the shape of the dunes facing the swale. Why is the color of the sand an important consideration affecting the temperature above it?

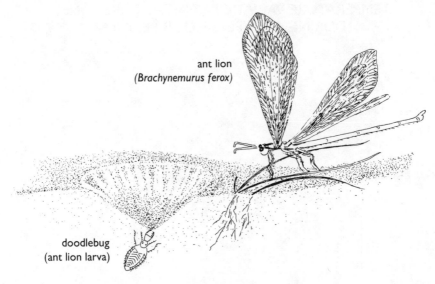

ant lion
(*Brachynemurus ferox*)

doodlebug
(ant lion larva)

Insects of the dunes

Animals and the Dunes. The animals that live in the dunes are almost all arthropods, such as insects and spiders, and many of them can be seen during the day. Dune-dwelling vertebrates like mice tend to stay in the cool protection of their burrows by day, venturing out only in the cool of the evening or before dawn. With the help of your field guide, find some of these curious dune dwellers. Velvet ants (which are really wasps), sand-dwelling grasshoppers, digger wasps, tiger beetles, and ant lions are only a few of these rugged insects.

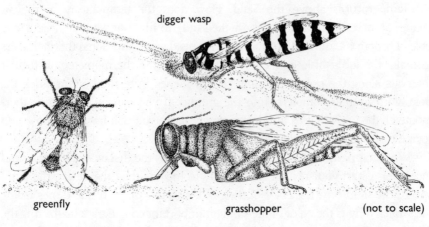

digger wasp

greenfly

grasshopper

(not to scale)

More insects of the dunes

THE BEACH

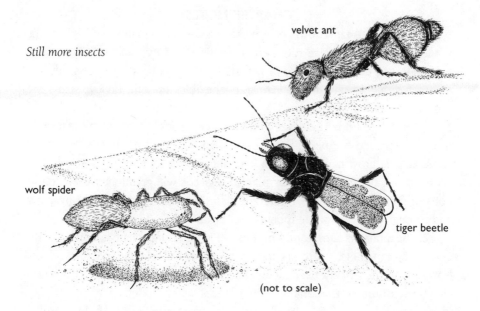

velvet ant

Still more insects

wolf spider

tiger beetle

(not to scale)

Take some time observing them and see if you can discover some of their survival adaptations. Many of these are behavioral as well as structural. (See Chapter Note 4 for some of these adaptations.)

If your search for animal life is in an area that has extensive dune fields, you will find evidence of the presence of a variety of species of higher animals, such as birds, snakes, lizards, turtles, raccoons, foxes, toads, meadow voles, and white-footed mice. However, you will not find frogs or worms. Why not?

ANIMAL ADAPTATIONS FOR LIFE ON THE DUNES

Animal	Adaptations	
	Behavioral	Structural
Ant lion		
Velvet ant		
Digger wasp		
Grasshopper		
Tiger beetle		
Green fly		
Wolf spider		
Miscellaneous		

CHAPTER NOTES

1. Sea Oat Adaptations. Like most grasses, these plants die back in the winter, but their extensive root system continues to live, and it will send up new shoots in the spring. Able to withstand dry periods, they flourish during summer droughts. The tough leaves and flexible, smooth, hollow stems are protection against stiff sea winds. Their root systems develop quickly and cover a lot of ground. The developing rhizomes quickly grow to six feet in all directions around the plant. Sand accumulation around the base of the plant stimulates its growth. Seeds of sea oats, the products of sexual reproduction, each contain an embryo, or baby plant. The seeds will germinate when conditions of moisture and temperature are right. The seeds are scattered by wind and through the feces of the rodents and birds that feed on them.

2. Adaptations Developed by Dune Plants. Dune plant adaptations include long tap roots, up to six feet in some sea oat plants, and thick, waxy leaves, as in the prickly pear cactus. Reduced leaves that resemble scales also effectively diminish evaporation. Tendrils that wind around other plants provide support for plants like beach pea. The hairs on the leaves of dusty miller reduce evaporation as well. Tiny, waxy leaves covered by a thick hairy coat serve the same purpose in beach heather. In general, the plants' above-ground structures tend to be reduced in size to further minimize water loss.

3. Temperature Variations on Dunes. The afternoon's onshore breezes are deflected by the crest of the primary dune so their cooling effect is lost to the region behind that dune. Radiation reflected from the back of the primary dune, the face of the secondary dune, and the small mounds of sand in the swale concentrate heat in this interdune region.

4. Insect Adaptations. Grasshoppers, tiger beetles, and digger wasps flee to the cooler air above the sand. The velvet ant is covered with tiny hairs that trap cooler air close to its body, allowing it to forage in the hot sand longer than other insects. The tiny, jointed legs of the tiger beetle are also covered with hairs that enable it to walk over hot sand and increase its dining time. Many insects simply burrow into the sand to escape the heat. The larvae of digger wasps, tiger beetles, and ant lions remain in burrows below the sand's surface. The wolf spider lines its burrow with silk for extra protection from the hot sun.

THE BEACH

CHAPTER 17

Tides

THE OCEAN'S PULSE

Will the moon be out tonight? Will it be a full moon, a half moon, or just a thin sliver of a moon? What time will the moon rise? Will there be a high tide this morning or this afternoon? Will the high tide be a regular high tide or a spring tide? These may seem like strange and unimportant questions in an age when our attention is more likely to be riveted on Monday night football, the ever present "impending world crisis" on the evening news, elections, the Olympics, and TV specials. Except for a few evening strollers or coastal fishermen, hardly anyone notices the moon or the tide.

Our grandfathers could probably answer questions about the moon and the tides, and so could their grandfathers back a hundred generations. Until very recently, the phases of the moon and the ebb and flow of the tide were an important part of daily life for mankind. For farming and hunting peoples, the passage of the moon through its phases marked off the year like a monthly calender in the sky. The moon signaled the time to plant and to hunt, the time to fish and to harvest. The moon was a source of myth and legend. The moon marked important religious events like Easter, Passover, and Ramadan.

The question "What time is high tide?" is as important today as it was in days past for those who live near the sea and draw their living from it and for those who enjoy catching an occasional seafood meal. Certain species of fish and crabs can be caught on the turn of the tide, while others are best caught at

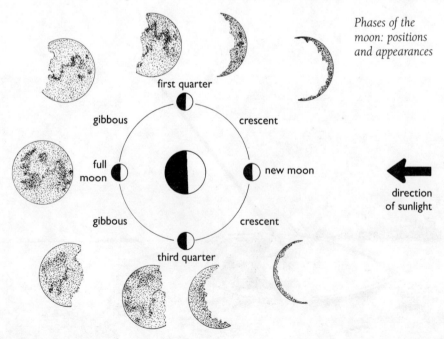

Phases of the moon: positions and appearances

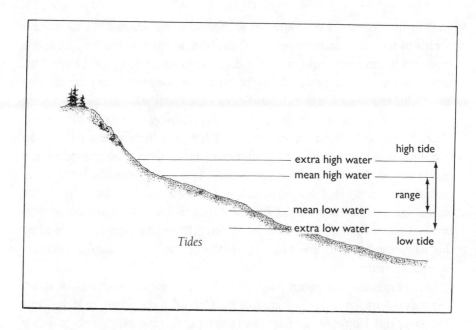

Tides

high tide. Before the advent of rail transport, highway systems, trucks, cars, buses, and planes, when the sea was the highway for all kinds of transport, the tides regulated the arrival and departure of people and goods.

Our ancestors not only routinely knew the current phase of the moon and the times of the local tides, they also understood that the questions we started with about the moon and the tides were related. They knew that when there was a full moon, the high tide was extra high and the low tide was extra low. They knew that the tides followed the lunar calendar, so that by knowing the phase of the moon, they could predict the time and height of tomorrow's tides. Many of the old clocks displayed the phase of the moon as well as the time of day. For many people today, this knowledge is lost. Did you know that the moon rises about fifty minutes later each day according to our twenty-four-hour solar clocks? Did you know that if there is a high tide this morning, the high tide tomorrow morning will be about fifty minutes later than it was today?

Ancient peoples had difficulty making sense of the connections between the moon and the tides. Three hundred years ago, Sir Isaac Newton gave us our modern understanding of tides by explaining that gravity is a force, a pull, exerted by every object on every other object. Huge objects exert huge pulling forces on each other. These forces keep the speeding planets in orbit around the sun and keep the moving moon in orbit around the earth. There is a balance between the attractive forces and the outward forces produced by the forward motion of the orbiting bodies. According to these ideas of Newton, the tides in the oceans of the earth result from the pull exerted on the earth's oceans by the moon and the sun. On the side of the earth facing the moon, this gravitational attraction pulls up a mound of water about half a yard high. This mound points toward the moon. As the earth spins one turn every twenty-four hours, this mound, or high tide, also circles the earth. This should give every point on the oceans one high tide each day. However, we know that many places have two high tides every day. This happens because our moon is so large that its pull on earth causes both moon and earth to whip around a point that is not at the center of the earth but offset about three thousand miles toward the moon. This whipping action causes a second tidal bulge in the oceans on exactly the opposite side of the earth from the gravitational tidal bulge. Presto, two high tides occur every day. The second high tide, caused by this whipping action, is lower than the high tide caused by the moon's gravitational attraction.

This explanation is based only on the fact that the earth rotates, or spins, and the explanation makes it seem that the high tides should arrive at the same time every day. However, we must also remember that the moon is not standing still in space. The moon is moving rapidly at about two thousand miles per hour, orbiting the spinning earth once every twenty-seven and one-half days. This fact causes the high tides to operate on the moon's schedule, which is about fifty minutes later every day for a given point on the earth. For example, if on some clear evening you see the moon rising like an enormous yellow orb on the eastern horizon, mark down the time. Then look in the same spot the following evening for Old Man Moon. You will find that moonrise is about fifty minutes later than it was the first evening. Since we have two high tides each day, there must be about twelve hours and twenty-five minutes between them.

There is another interesting thing about the tides that needs an explanation. During the lunar month of about twenty-nine and one-half days, there are two higher-than-usual high tides called spring tides, which occur at full moon and at new moon. There are also two lower-than-usual high tides called neap tides, which occur at the first and third quarters of the lunar cycle. The spring

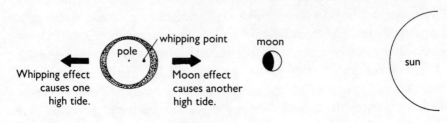

Two high tides daily

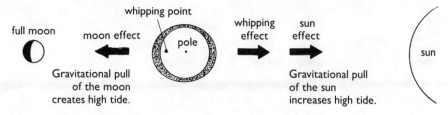

Spring tide: earth between sun and moon

tides are called this because the extrahigh water level at that time looks as though the water is "springing" from the earth. Spring tides have nothing to do with the spring season of the year. They are caused by the relative positions of the earth, sun, and moon, when they are lined up. The word *neap*, which comes from the German word for napping, is used to describe those tides in which there is very little movement of water. The water is "taking a snooze" at neap high tide.

Newton comes to the rescue here also. This spring-neap cycle is due to the gravitational attraction of the sun on the earth and its waters. The sun also exerts a gravitational pull on earth, causing a 46 percent smaller tidal bulge in the oceans. This does not result in another set of high tides; instead, it causes a tide that adds to, or reinforces, the moon tide when moon, earth, and sun are lined up. This additive tide is spring tide. When earth, moon, and sun are at right angles in space, then the smaller sun tide partially cancels the moon tide, resulting in neap tide.

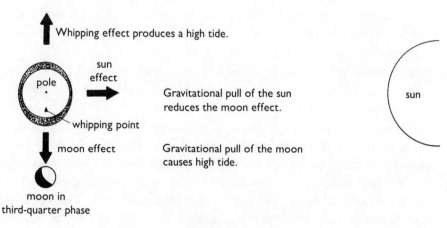

Neap tide

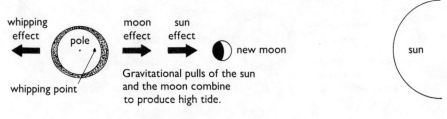

whipping effect

pole

whipping point

moon effect

sun effect

new moon

Gravitational pulls of the sun and the moon combine to produce high tide.

sun

Spring tide: moon between earth and sun

That might seem to be the whole story of the tides, a complete explanation; however, the story is complicated by the weird shapes of the solid parts of the earth's surface. In New York City there is approximately a five-foot difference between low and high tides, while Rockport, Maine, has a ten-foot tidal range, and the Bay of Fundy boasts a more-than-thirty-foot tide. The very uneven coastline causes these variations. Almost anywhere you travel, you will find strange things about local tides if you ask a fisherman or someone who lives on the shore. Most places have two high tides per day, but some communities, like Pensacola, Florida, on the Gulf of Mexico, have only one high tide per day, and San Francisco has one big high tide and one little high tide every day. These strange effects are also due to the way the land masses interact with tidal movements.

It may seem odd, but far out at sea, the effects of the tide cause a bulge in the surface of the ocean, which people on ships cannot notice. For a few hours each day, the ship is half a yard closer to the moon, and then six hours later, half a yard farther from the moon. When the tidal bulge reaches shallow water, there may be a great rush of water into the bays, sounds, and estuaries. These tidal currents can be very powerful, and they move gigantic quantities of water in a daily rhythm. Man has dreamed of using this movement of water to produce useful power. This is done now on a small scale, but the harmful ecological effects of using this power on a large scale may outweigh the potential savings in oil and coal.

Since every aspect of planet earth is intimately associated with living things, the tides have an important life-related role. With each rise of the tide, nutrients generated in the oceans are brought into bays, into estuaries, and even into the smallest of tidal creeks. Similarly, the falling tide carries with it food matter originating in marshlands, mud flats, and rivers. The churning associated with tidal shifts moves this food material vertically as well as horizontally. The beat of life in the intertidal zone is directed by tidal motion.

THE BEACH

When you think of it, there is no aspect of planet earth that is not intimately bound up with the teeming miracle of life. Even the ancient partnership between the earth and the moon provides a kind of life pulse that goes on and on. We are all part of this pulsating rhythm, part of this eternal beat.

THE WORLD OF TIDES

What you will need

basic kit
watch
rubber bands
camera
drawing paper
tall sticks or broom handles
graph paper
weather page from a local
  newspaper
tide tables

Science skills

observing
measuring
graphing
inferring

OBSERVATIONS

Although coastal profiles change with the rise and fall of the tides, we are often unaware of how different a beach looks during the different phases of the tidal cycle. Rocks of assorted sizes, hidden by the waters of high tide, are exposed at low tide, while a large expanse of beach can practically disappear at high tide. If you visit several different coastal areas and take pictures at high tide and again at low tide, you can begin a pictorial record of these changes. It is essential for you to take the pictures from the same place on each beach at both high and low tides. If you prefer, you can make drawings instead of taking photos of the beaches. Regardless of the method you choose to record the changes in the shape of the shoreline, be sure you include in your records the name of the beach, date, time, phase of the moon, and weather conditions.

EXPLORATIONS

These activities are best thought of as part of a day at the beach. They should fit in with the other enjoyable things that make the beach such a treat for everyone. If you are visiting a beach area for the first time, or if you are making your first observations of a familiar beach, you should get a copy of the local newspaper. There is often information about local tides on the weather page of the newspaper. Find the times of local high and low tides. What other information about tides does the paper give? Does your paper give the tidal range for the day – the difference between the highest high tide and the lowest low tide? Does the paper provide information on the phases of the moon?

Which Way Is the Water Moving? When you go to the beach, bring a stick about five feet long. A broom handle with one end sharpened will do nicely. Find a place that is away from the crowds and away from swimmers. Pound the stick firmly into the sand at the water's edge with a rock, and with a rubber band, mark the stick at the level of the water (the highest wet spot will do). Record the time and wait a little while. Then check the water level on your stick. Is the tide flooding (coming in) or is the tide ebbing (going out)? How does your finding compare with the information in your newspaper?

A Falling Tide. If the tide is falling, place your stick at the highest spot reached by the most recent wave. Then keep moving your stick back to the edge of the water every half hour. Observe the time when the tide stops falling. Was there an in-between time when the tide stayed quiet without moving out or moving in? (See Chapter Note 1 for ideas on the uneven movement of the tides.) Note the time when the tide begins to move in. How do the times you have recorded compare with the time of the low tide given in the newspaper?

A Rising Tide. As the tide rises, use your supply of rubber bands to mark the height of the tide on your stick every half hour. You will want to keep track of the time as each new rubber band goes in place until the tide reaches its highest mark. How high is the high tide above the low tide? What portion of its total rise did the tide rise the first hour, second hour, and third hour? Did the tide rise evenly or in spurts? At what portion of the tidal cycle was the maximum rate of rise? What happened to the rate of tidal rise during the next three hours?

Tide Tables. Professional fishermen, weekend anglers, and clam diggers know that high and low tides do not occur at the same time every day. The easiest way to find the times of the high and low tides is to use a tide table. These tables are often offered free by the local bait and tackle shop or by a boating supply store. You can also buy tide tables for any locality for the entire year. For the purposes of this activity, you can use the following sample excerpt from a tide table. (See Chapter Note 2 for directions on how to order your own tide tables.)

Notice that the time columns show hours and minutes and are given according to a twenty-four-hour clock. This clock begins at midnight (0000 hours) and continues around the clock for twenty-four hours. Therefore, instead of starting the time cycle over at noon, you simply continue counting around the clock until you reached 2400 hours (which is also 0000 hours), or twelve midnight.

NEW YORK, N.Y., THE BATTERY

TIME MERIDIAN 75°W
ADD 1 HOUR FOR DAYLIGHT SAVING TIME

APRIL

	Time	Height (feet)		Time	Height (feet)		Time	Height (feet)		Time	Height (feet)
1	0331	4.5	**9**	0439	−0.5	**16**	0510	4.3	**24**	0419	0.3
	1025	0.5		1055	4.6		1123	0.4		1013	3.9
Sa	1620	4.1	Su	1643	0.0	Su	1740	4.5	M	1555	0.8
	2241	0.6		2316	5.5		2348	0.6		2208	4.9
2	0444	4.7	**10**	0533	−0.1	**17**	0558	4.4	**25**	0451	0.5
	1116	0.1		1152	4.3		1206	0.3		1054	3.8
Su	1723	4.6	M	1736	0.4	M	1822	4.8	Tu	1627	0.9
	2339	0.1		−	−		−	−		2255	4.8
3	0544	5.0	**11**	0013	5.2	**18**	0032	0.4	**26**	0531	0.7
	1206	−0.2		0633	0.3		0640	4.5		1146	3.7
M	1815	5.2	Tu	1252	4.1	Tu	1246	0.2	W	1704	1.0
	−	−		1842	0.8		1901	5.0		2349	4.7
4	0032	−0.3	**12**	0111	4.8	**19**	0115	0.2	**27**	0623	0.8
	0635	5.2		0743	0.6		0717	4.6		1245	3.8
Tu	1253	−0.5	W	1351	4.0	W	1325	0.2	Th	1759	1.2
	1902	5.6		1958	1.1		1933	5.1		−	−
5	0123	−0.6	**13**	0210	4.5	**20**	0154	0.1	**28**	0052	4.6
	0725	5.4		0851	0.7		0754	4.5		0742	0.8
W	1340	−0.7	Th	1453	3.9	Th	1401	0.2	F	1345	4.0
	1949	6.0		2112	1.1		2008	5.1		1947	1.2
6	0214	−0.9	**14**	0312	4.3	**21**	0234	0.1	**29**	0156	4.6
	0813	5.4		0948	0.6		0828	4.4		0855	0.7
Th	1426	−0.8	F	1554	4.0	F	1436	0.3	Sa	1446	4.2
	2036	6.1		2210	1.0		2037	5.1		2118	1.0
7	0303	−0.9	**15**	0412	4.3	**22**	0310	0.1	**30**	0303	4.6
	0903	5.2		1039	0.5		0902	4.3		0951	0.4
F	1511	−0.7	Sa	1652	4.2	Sa	1505	0.5	Su	1551	4.6
	2126	6.0		2302	0.8		2105	5.1		2220	0.6
8	0350	−0.8				**23**	0345	0.2			
	0957	4.9					0936	4.1			
Sa	1557	−0.4				Su	1533	0.6			
	2219	5.8					2135	5.0			

The time columns above give high water and low water in correct time sequence. The height columns show whether this is high or low water time; 0000 is midnight, 1200 is noon. Heights are reckoned from the datum of soundings on charts of the locality, which is mean lower low water.

Reading the Tables. How many high and low tides are there in a twenty-four-hour period? (See Chapter Note 3 for more information on tides and tables.)

Using the sample tide information, determine the time of high tide on the evening of Saturday, April 1. What is the height in feet of that high tide? At what time does high tide occur on the evening of Tuesday, April 18? Is that a higher high tide than the tide on April 1?

Graph a Tidal Cycle. The graph shows the height in feet of high tide and of low tide for the Battery in New York for April 1989. It shows clearly the

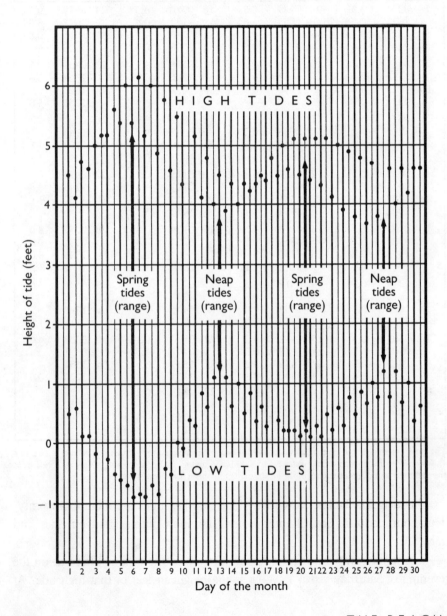

THE BATTERY
New York, NY   April 1989

THE BEACH

progression of spring and neap tides during the month. The graph also shows that the high tides each day are not equally high. The higher tide is caused by the gravitational force, and the lower high tide is caused by the whipping action explained earlier in this chapter. Using this graph as a guide and using local tide tables, make a graph of the tides in your area for a month. What days had spring tides (exceptionally high tides) and what days had neap tides (smaller than average high tides)? In order to determine the role of the moon in the tidal drama, keep a record of its phases.

Tidal Effects on Life. The information you have plotted on your graph can be used to answer some interesting questions. On what dates would you expect to find the red seaweeds exposed at the time of very low tide? On what dates would you expect the meadows of *Spartina patens* to be flooded by extra-high tidal waters? (See Chapter Note 4 for an explanation.)

CHAPTER NOTES

1. **The Uneven Coming and Going of the Tide.** The amount of horizontal rise in tidal water follows a fairly regular pattern. In the first hour, the tide will rise only very slightly; during the second hour, it will move quite noticeably; and during the third hour (at half tide), the rate is at its maximum. Then the amount of rise each hour decreases until the sixth hour, when its rise is again hardly noticeable. The falling tide shows the same pattern: the tide falls slowly at first, then more rapidly, and then slowly again.

2. **Sources for Tide Charts.** Tide charts are published by the National Oceanographic and Atmospheric Administration of the United States Department of Commerce (NOAA). You can request these tables from the United States Government Printing Office, North Capitol and H Streets, N.W., Washington, D.C. 20401 (202-275-2051). These same charts and brief excerpts from them are often available in marine supply stores, bait shops, coastal book stores, hardware stores, banks, marine insurance offices, and other unexpected places. Some of these tables have more information than others, so check them out carefully.

3. **High and Low Water.** There are two high tides and two low tides in a twenty-four-hour period. This tidal pattern is called semidiurnal, and it occurs on the Atlantic and Pacific coasts of the United States.

4. **Some Plants and the Tide.** *Chondrus crispus* and other red seaweeds live below the mean low water, so they are exposed only during the spring tides. *Spartina patens* lives in that portion of the salt marsh that is flooded only during the spring tides. This flooding is essential since *Spartina patens* seeds will not germinate unless flooded by seawater.

Selected Bibliography

THE ROCKY SHORE

Abbott, Isabella, and E. Yale Dawson. *How to Know the Seaweeds*. Dubuque, Iowa: William C. Brown Co., 1978.

Dawson, E. Yale. *Marine Botany: An Introduction*. New York: Holt, Rinehart and Winston, Inc., 1966.

Kingsbury, John M. *Seaweeds: Cape Cod and the Islands*. Chatham, Massachusetts: Chatham Press, 1969.

Lack, Larry. "Cultured Mussels Could Benefit Maine." *National Fisherman* 63 (November 1982): 28-31.

Lee, Thomas. *The Seaweed Handbook: An Illustrated Guide to Seaweeds from North Carolina to the Arctic*. New York: Dover Publications, Inc., 1986.

Lehman, Phyllis. "Barnacles." *National Wildlife* 22 (August-September 1984): 20-25.

McHugh, J.L. "Whales Have Riders Too." *Sea Frontiers* 32 (July-August 1986): 252-260.

Mangin, Katrinia. "A Pox upon the Rocks: A Newcomer Clears a Place for Itself along a Crowded Rock Shore." *Natural History* 99 (June 1990): 50-54.

Olander, Doug. "The Misunderstood Mussel." *Sea Frontiers* 26 (July–August 1980): 205–212.

Stuller, Jay. "Mussel Colonies Thrive on Oil Platform Legs." *Oceans* (January-February 1987): 6-10.

Sze, Philip. *A Biology of the Algae*. Dubuque, Iowa: William C. Brown Publishers, 1986.

THE SALT MARSH AND THE MUD FLATS

Barlow, Roger B., Jr. "What the Brain Tells the Eye." *Scientific American* 262 (April 1990): 90-96.

Carty, Winthrop P. "Birds of a Feather Feed Together." *Americas* 39 (September-October 1987): 28-29.

Filisky, Michael. *Peterson First Guides: Fishes*. Boston: Houghton Mifflin Co., 1989.

Kelley, Ken. "Horseshoe Crab Soars from Pest to Resource." *National Fisherman* 65 (February 1985): 26-28.

Moyle, Peter B., and Joseph J. Cech, Jr. *Fishes: An Introduction to Ichthyology*. Englewood Cliffs, New Jersey: Prentice-Hall, Inc., 1988.

Myers, J.P. "Sex and Gluttony on Delaware Bay." *Natural History* 95 (May 1986): 68-78.

Richards, Alan. *Shorebirds: A Complete Guide to Their Behavior and Migration*. New York: W.H. Smith Publishers, Inc., 1988.

Robins, C. Richard. *A Field Guide to Atlantic Coast Fishes of North America*. Boston: Houghton Mifflin Co., 1986.

Teal, John, and Mildred Teal. *Life and Death of the Salt Marsh*. Boston: Little, Brown & Co., 1969.

THE BEACH

Beatty, J. Kelley. "A Once-Closer Relative." *Sky and Telescope* 68 (November 1984): 392.

Brogdon, Bill. "Pinpointing Local Tide Predictions." *Motor Boating and Sailing* 156 (December 1985): 66-68.

Hoel, Michael. *Land's Edge: A Natural History of Barrier Beaches from Maine to North Carolina*. Chester, Connecticut: Globe Pequot, 1986.

Hoyt, John. *Field Guide to the Beaches*. Boston: Houghton Mifflin Co., 1971.

Ranwell, D.S. *Ecology of Salt Marshes and Sand Dunes*. London: Chapman and Hall, 1972.

Trefil, James S. *A Scientist at the Seashore*. New York: Charles Scribner, 1984.

Wood, Amos L. *Beachcombing the Pacific*. West Chester, Pennsylvania: Schiffer Publishing, Ltd., 1987.

FIELD GUIDES

Berrill, Deborah, and Michael Berrill. *The Atlantic Coast: Cape Cod to Newfoundland*. San Francisco: Sierra Club Books, 1981.

Eschmeyer, William N., and Earl S. Herald. *Field Guide to Pacific Coast Fishes: North America from the Gulf of Alaska to Baja California*. Boston: Houghton Mifflin Co., 1983.

Farrand, John, Jr., ed. *The Audubon Society Master Guide to Birding*. Vol. 1-3. New York: Alfred A. Knopf, 1983.

Fotheringham, Nick. *Beachcombers Guide to Gulf Coast Marine Life*. Houston, Texas: Gulf Coast Publishing Co., 1980.

Gosner, Kenneth. *A Field Guide to the Atlantic Seashore*. Boston: Houghton Mifflin, 1979.

McConnaughey, Bayard, and Evelyn McConnaughey. *Audubon Society Nature Guides: Pacific Coast*. New York: Alfred A. Knopf, 1988.

Perry, Bill. *The Middle Atlantic Coast: Cape Hatteras to Cape Cod*. San Francisco: Sierra Club Books, 1985.

Pough, Frederick H. *A Field Guide to Rocks and Minerals*. Boston: Houghton Mifflin Co., 1976.

Robbins, Chandler S. *Birds of North America*. New York: Golden Press, 1983.

White, Christopher P. *Chesapeake Bay: A Field Guide*. Centreville, Maryland: Tidewater Publishers, 1989.

GENERAL INTEREST

Berrill, N.J., and Jacquelyn Berrill. *1001 Questions Answered about the Seashore*. New York: Dover Publications, Inc., 1976.

Borror, Donald. *Dictionary of Word Roots and Combining Forms*. Palo Alto, California: Mayfield Publishing Co., 1971.

Buchsbaum, Ralph Morris. *Animals without Backbones*. Chicago: University of Chicago Press, 1987.

Carefoot, Thomas. *Pacific Seashores: A Guide to Intertidal Ecology*. Seattle: University of Washington Press, 1977.

Fox, William. *At the Sea's Edge*. Englewood Cliffs, New Jersey: Prentice-Hall, 1983.

Lerman, Matthew. *Marine Diversity: Environment, Diversity and Ecology*. Menlo Park, California: The Benjamin Cummings Publishing Company, Inc., 1986.

Milne, Lorus. *Invertebrates of North America*. New York: Doubleday, 1972.

Solem, George Allen. *The Shell Makers: Introducing the Mollusks*. New York: Wiley, 1974.

Sumich, James L. *An Introduction to the Biology of Marine Life*. Dubuque, Iowa: William C. Brown Co., 1980.

Teal, John, and Mildred Teal. *Life and Death of the Salt Marsh*. Boston: Little, Brown & Co., 1969.

Warner, William W. *Beautiful Swimmer: Waterman, Crabs and Chesapeake Bay*. Boston: Little, Brown & Co., 1976.

NOTES

NOTES